Praise for
Intangible Assets

"Cohen has produced a broad, engaging, and admirably clear discussion of intangible assets and their valuation. There is useful background here for thinking about diverse areas of the law—in addition to obvious applications in intellectual property, corporate, and securities law, one thinks of, for example, administrative law, where debates about cost-benefit analysis ranging over intangible (and often ephemeral) assets are both ubiquitous and contentious. A good and helpful book."

—Daniel J. Gilman, J.D., PhD
University of Maryland School of Law

"Cohen does a superb job in effectively communicating the essence of the value of intangible assets-something you can't see, touch, or smell, yet clearly important to companies and the management of their balance sheets. This insightful book will both clarify the notion of intangible asset valuation to the interested amateur and provide guidance to the knowledgeable professional. Well written with real world examples, *Intangible Assets* will provide a solid background on this interesting and well-debated practice, and should be required reading for anyone desiring the complete picture on asset valuation."

—Kris S. Larsen
Managing Director
Interbrand Wood Healthcare

"Cohen has presented the law, accounting, and economics of intellectual property with clarity and precision."

—Ram Shivakumar
Adjunct Professor of Economics and Strategy
Graduate School of Business, University of Chicago

"Cohen has a knack of making complex topics easily understandable. I learn something new every time I pick up the book. This is a book that I will keep on my bookshelf for easy reference."

—Jeffrey Seifman
Partner
Kirkland & Ellis

Intangible Assets

Valuation and Economic Benefit

JEFFREY A. COHEN

John Wiley & Sons, Inc.

Copyright © 2005 by Jeffrey A. Cohen. All rights reserved

Published by John Wiley & Sons, Inc., Hoboken, New Jersey.

Published simultaneously in Canada.

For general information about our other products and services, please contact our Customer Care Department within the United States at 800-762-2974, outside the United States at 317-572-3993 or fax 317-572-4002.

Wiley also publishes its books in a variety of electronic formats. Some content that appears in print may not be available in electronic books. For more information about Wiley products, visit our Web site at www.wiley.com.

Library of Congress Cataloging-in-Publication Data

Cohen, Jeffrey A., 1964–
    Intangible assets : valuation and economic benefit / Jeffrey A. Cohen.
        p. cm. — (Wiley finance series)
    Includes bibliographical references and index.
    ISBN 0-471-67131-2 (CLOTH)
    1. Intangible property—Economic aspects. 2. Intangible property—Accounting. 3. Corporations—Valuation. I. Title. II. Series.
    HF5681.I55C64 2005
    658.15—dc22

                                    2004021907

Printed in the United States of America

10 9 8 7 6 5 4 3 2 1

*This book is for all of my family, who provide
the most important intangible asset unconditionally.*

Contents

Preface

Valuing things we cannot touch is both an esoteric endeavor and a commonplace act. It occurs in almost every area of daily economic life. For example, would a couple going into a restaurant rather have a quiet table now in the smoking section, or would they prefer to wait for one near the kitchen door? The answer will be different depending on their preferences. Are they in a hurry? Are they smokers? Do they mind the noise near the kitchen?

The chief executive officer (CEO) of a pharmaceutical corporation may want to know how much a particular portfolio of drug patents is worth because a competitor is interested in buying the patents. Should he sell? At what price? Under what circumstances? The CEO needs to know the value of these intangible assets.

At the same time, a family might be thinking of sending their daughter off to college. The parents might ask whether it is worth spending $30,000 a year for a private university, or whether the local public college at $7,000 per year is good enough. In this context, what does "worth" even mean? And "good enough" to what end? It is the value of her education the parents wish to measure, and that is certainly an intangible asset.

So how can we talk about things as different as a portfolio of pharmaceutical patents and a student's college education in the same breath? The answer is that in each instance, the decision requires an analysis of the costs and benefits, and that process is at the root of economic reasoning. We choose the path that we hope will produce more return, earn more benefits, make more money, and give greater satisfaction than the other path.

What further links these assets together is that neither one—the patents or the eventual bachelor's degree—are physical assets. To be sure, both possess some tangible characteristics, but the paper on which they are written is not what makes them valuable. Ownership of the property rights associated with each asset—the right to manufacture a particular drug, or the right to claim graduating from a particular school, or the knowledge acquired, or the networking opportunities created—is what is important. That ownership right is valuable when the drug is successful, or when the student succeeds because of the schooling.

This book presents a comprehensive framework for thinking about all intangible assets, from patents to education, from brands to goodwill. It is not confined to assets that can be bought or sold, although that is sometimes a useful distinction to make. The scope is wide: Many things are intangibles, and at least a reasonable attempt should be made to capture the important ones in a valuation. This book presents the concept of a firm's portfolio of intangible economic benefits—PIE-B, for short—a basket that includes items not listed in the firm's accounting records and often overlooked by valuation analysts. What goes into the basket are a little like proto-assets—nebulous to a degree, but still based on some positive ownership and economic benefit.

The identification of intangibles is a central theme in this book. Sometimes identifying a firm's intangible assets is hard, but valuing them is easy. Other times just the opposite is the case. Identification is largely what makes valuing intangible assets different from valuing tangible or physical assets. For analysts or managers, finding and quantifying the intangible assets of a firm improves the valuation, whether that valuation supports a transaction, litigation, or strategic improvement of the firm's operations.

Despite the broad discussion of different types of intangibles, this book is not a treatise on intangible asset valuation. There are good books and academic work in economics, accounting, finance, and valuation that go into greater detail of analysis; many of these works are cited as references. This book is intended for business students, management professionals, and attorneys who want a comprehensive introduction to valuing intangible assets. It will help readers find intangibles, especially those not on a company's balance sheet, and it will help readers value those intangibles.

Most important, readers of this book will learn that even when intangibles are hard to spot, and even if they are harder to value, the endeavor should not be abandoned. As the old saying goes, getting there is half the fun.

Jeffrey A. Cohen
Chicago 2004

Acknowledgments

This book could not have been written without the influence and help of numerous friends and colleagues. Though their views were indispensable, all errors or omissions remain solely my own. My colleagues at Chicago Partners, especially Bob Topel and Jonathan Arnold, have helped form the bedrock of my own economic thinking. Steve Basileo, Stuart McCrary (who got me into this), Ricardo Cossa, and John Szoboscan provided many helpful comments on earlier drafts. Special thanks goes to Robert Riley and Claire Anderson, who contributed exceptional research assistance.

CHAPTER 1

Introducing Intangibles

All firms, no matter how big or how small they are, have both tangible and intangible assets. The desks, computers, factories, and inventory of a business are certainly tangible assets. At the same time, firms might possess some well-known intangibles—assets such as patents, copyrights, contractual obligations, customer lists, or other intellectual property. Many of these intangible assets show up on firms' financial statements.

But firms might possess another kind of intangible asset, one that is harder to classify and value. Perhaps a company has long-established customers, or exclusive supplier agreements, an experienced and loyal workforce, a great location, or a chief operating officer with superlative organizational skills. These are surely assets, but they cannot be touched or felt, and they probably do not appear anywhere on the company's financial statements. How can they be valued?

HOW THIS BOOK IS ORGANIZED

This book is organized into 11 chapters. The remainder of Chapter 1 provides an overview as well as a brief introduction to the theory of the three main valuation approaches: income, market, and cost.

Chapter 2 presents the taxonomy and historical context of intangible assets. This chapter introduces readers to the classification and nomenclature generally found in the literature on intangibles.

Chapter 3 covers the economics of intangibles, measurements of their growth, and selected research data. It discusses the efforts that accountants and economists have made to understand why intangibles matter and how they affect value.

Chapter 4 presents a summary of the latest accounting methodology and rules for the treatment of intangible assets under generally accepted accounting principles (GAAP). Topics include revenue recognition, asset impairment, amortization, and remaining useful life. As we shall see, the new accounting rules can have a large effect on a firm's treatment of intangibles.

Chapter 5 introduces the idea of a firm's portfolio of intangible economic benefits (PIE-B). In this chapter, the conceptual jumping-off point for the remainder of the book, the process of identifying intangibles takes center stage.

Chapter 6 begins the presentation of valuation methods, starting with the income approach. This chapter introduces the discounted cash flow (DCF) methodology and applies it to intangible assets. It also presents an options valuation method.

Chapter 7 presents the second common valuation method, which uses comparable assets, companies, and "market multiples" to benchmark the value of an intangible. This method is sometimes called the market method because the appraiser considers how the market will value similar assets.

Chapter 8 presents the third common valuation method, the calculation of the cost of the intangible asset. This chapter discusses book cost, replacement cost, and the functionally equivalent or "design-around" cost of intangible assets.

Chapter 9 shows some of the ways intangibles are valued in litigation. The so-called Panduit test, the horizontal merger guidelines, and the Georgia Pacific factors provide useful frameworks for thinking about the valuation of intangibles in terms of lost profits, market definition, and reasonable royalty calculation. The chapter also discusses important recent trademark law.

Chapter 10 discusses strategy and securitization of intangibles.

Chapter 11 presents a theory of ephemeral assets.

WHAT IS VALUATION ANYWAY?

According to *Merriam Webster's Collegiate Dictionary*, value can be defined as "1: a fair return or equivalent in goods, services, or money for something exchanged; 2: the monetary worth of something: marketable price; 3: relative worth, utility, or importance."[1] As we shall see, the concepts of a fair return, the marketable price, relative worth, or utility are central to the three basic valuation methodologies. But before we begin looking at intangibles in earnest, it is worth spending a little time considering the concept of value. After all, there are valuation experts, valuation and appraisal societies, and Web sites devoted to nothing but this mysterious black box called valuation.

Let us start with something tangible. Suppose that you own a car that you wish to sell yourself, perhaps in the local newspaper, and you want to know how much to ask; that is, you want to know its value. Suppose, further, that it is a 1997 silver Toyota Camry, with 50,000 miles. The first thing you might do is look up what a third-party source, such as *Kelley Blue Book* or the National Automobile Dealers Association, reports for a car like yours in the same condition with the same set of options. The source might report a private party value of $5,000. How does it arrive at this amount?

Market Approach

Automobile valuation guides examine comparables. Used-car evaluators would likely look at retail and wholesale sales prices of other 1997 Toyota Camrys with the same mileage, or they may construct comparable sales transactions, say, from other Japanese-branded sedans, or other 1997 cars, or other Toyotas, or other cars with about 50,000 miles. They probably will take into account the color, too. (Generally, used green cars sell at a greater discount!) The sales that are economically comparable give a pretty good indication of what your Toyota is worth. Why? Because if prospective buyers are interested in your car, they should be willing to pay only the market price; and the value in a trade now should closely resemble prices from the recent past.

This simple example introduces in a general way the concept of *market efficiency*. If you try to ask much more than $5,000 for your car, and potential buyers know what other like cars are selling for (and there is no shortage of similar cars), those buyers simply will buy the silver Camry down the block. The fact that other cars just like yours sell for around $5,000 limits any premium you may be able to get. There may be other reasons that you can charge more than similar cars for sale; in fact, there may be intangibles associated with your car, but let us not complicate things too much just yet.

The *Blue Book* evaluators may also report a wholesale price or a trade-in price that is less than the retail $5,000. These prices reflect different transactions. Dealers who think they can sell your car to someone else or are willing to take your car in trade when you buy a new car from them are working with a different set of assumptions, a different equation for considering what your car is worth *to them*. For example, they might need to recondition your car in order to sell it to someone else. This might cost them $500, so they would be willing to pay you at most $4,500. Or they might be willing to give you the full $5,000 because they are going to make it up on the sale of a new car to you.

These alternative prices introduce a couple of additional important valuation concepts. First is that valuation must reflect value *to someone*. In other words, the asset's value is in the context of a transaction. For example, what do the prospective buyers want to do with the asset? Are they under pressure to buy fast? A young couple eloping that very night face a different set of transportation constraints than, say, a casual shopper looking for second family car.

Second, the transaction inherently reflects costs-benefits analysis. In our example, the car dealers are thinking about (at least) these inputs:

- Whether you know what your car is worth to a private party
- How much it might cost them to recondition your car for sale
- How likely they will be able to sell your car in an acceptable amount of time
- Whether they are giving up a better opportunity for the use of cash
- Whether you are going to purchase a new car from them at the same time

At the end of the day, if they will make money on the entire transaction the dealers should be willing to do the deal. In the terminology of finance, car dealers should be calculating the *net present value* of the deal, and the basis for their valuation is the analysis of what the market will bear—hence, this approach is called the market approach to valuation. (We will discuss net present value more in Chapter 6 and the market approach in Chapter 7.)

One last comment on valuation through comparables: It need not require the advice or analysis of third parties, such as car appraisers in the previous example. You might just as easily look in the newspaper yourself or go online to auction sites such as eBay to determine the market price, although of course you will need to consider that the newspaper listings and reserve prices on eBay are asking prices, not transaction prices.

Income Approach

The market approach to valuing the car may seem the most intuitive. But it is not necessarily correct. In fact, it would be wrong in the next context.

Suppose that you and your neighbor are both applying for a temporary job as a pizza delivery person. Your potential employer will pay you the same hourly rate and also will pay for your gas. In all regards you and your neighber are equally qualified for the job. The only difference is that she drives a gas guzzler that gets 10 miles per gallon while your Toyota gets 25. Now, the value of your car to your potential employer has little to do with the value we calculated in the sales example. The pizzeria owner is not interested in buying a car; he is interested in how much two different cars will cost him.

The right valuation in this case would be based on the income approach. From the employer's perspective, the calculation is simply how much more hiring your neighbor will cost than hiring you, or, alternatively, how much more he will make by hiring you. In other words, he is calculating different income streams based on the fuel efficiency of the two different cars.

For simplification, let us suppose that the job is going to require 1,000 miles of driving and gas is $1 per gallon. If the pizzeria owner hires you, it will cost him $40 in gas, versus $100 if he hires your neighbor. In this context, your car is valued at $60 more than your neighbor's. (This simple example ignores any discount for the fact that in either case, the cost of fuel is spread out over time.)

Cost Approach

Let us think about one more approach to valuing the car. Suppose for a moment that you have been involved in an accident in which your car has been badly damaged. The other party is at fault, and the person's insurance company has agreed to cover the "value" of your loss. In this context, that value could have different definitions. It might be the cost to repair your car. The damage may be $3,000 to fix, making your car worth only $2,000. The value of the insurance policy is $3,000 if it covers the value of the loss as measured by repair cost.

Value might mean the cost to replace the car with another silver Toyota Camry. Depending on how the insurance policy is written, that replacement cost could be the cost of a new Toyota, or perhaps the policy specifies that you will be entitled only to a car of similar year, make, and model to your loss. If there really are a lot of similar Camrys in the market, that replacement cost is going to be identical to the value derived under the market approach. The repair cost, however, could even exceed the replacement cost.

The point here, again, is not to assume that all valuation roads lead to Rome. The context of a transaction or the meaning of a contract can imply very different asset valuations. As we will soon see, these three basic valuation approaches—market, income, and cost—are the same tools we use in analyzing the value of intangible assets.

Arm's-Length Transactions

In many valuations, the terms "arm's-length negotiation" or "arm's-length transaction" are invoked. These terms mean that a transaction taking place is between two unrelated parties, or at least two parties who are trying to maximize their side of the bargain. This does not mean that each party has equal information about what an asset is worth; in other words, there can be *information asymmetry*. Indeed, because intangibles often are harder to value than tangibles, information asymmetry plays an important role in negotiating acquisitions where intangibles loom large. But to be at arms' length, whatever price eventually is reached is not the result of a nonmarket relationship or agreement between the two parties. A simple exception is when a parent sells the family home to a child for a price below market. An intangible asset example might be when a corporation licenses at a heavy discount some piece of intellectual property, such as a trademark, to a sub-sidiary or franchisee.

Appraisals and Fairness Opinions

Often appraisals and valuations are discussed at the same time. For pur-poses of this book, we consider appraisals and appraisal techniques to be a type of valuation, largely confined to tangible assets and, in particular, real estate. This is not to say that a real estate appraiser goes through a differ-ent analysis than does someone valuing a firm's copyrights, for example. In fact, the two evaluators may both consider market, income, and cost approaches. Nonetheless, appraisal institutes (i.e., the American Society of Appraisers) and their members often have specific procedural steps that characterize their work; those features may not apply to the general eco-nomic analysis that this book seeks to describe.

Similarly, the parties in a transaction often seek a fairness opinion. Financial institutions that are party to a deal often require such an opinion; they seek either explicit indemnification or just comfort that the deal passes legal and accounting tests, and they bring in an outside accountant to undertake the analysis. The fairness opinion also is based on certain stan-dards that, although not at odds with the general approach considered here, are for the most part better left for a separate discussion.

Individuals as Economic Units

Most valuations are done when some interested party is contemplating buy-ing a firm or part of a firm. This book is concerned primarily with valuing the intangibles that reside in the business that is under consideration. But the overarching theme of this book is that people possess intangibles, too, and that valuation of intangibles need not stop at the firm level. We might even consider a little economic theory here. The Nobel Prize–winning econ-omist Ronald Coase posited in 1937 in *The Nature of the Firm* that a firm's boundaries were determined by the cost to contract externally for goods with another firm versus production in-house.[2] We shall adopt this same principle and will apply the techniques in this book to individuals and the transactions we as individuals contemplate—for instance, the college education discussed earlier. The text that follows may describe a firm, but readers should remember that each of us operates at least one firm made up of our own personal collection of tangible and intangible assets.

The Hypotheticals

One last introductory note: Many of the examples in this text are admittedly and purposefully simplifications of various principles. The economic, accounting, and financial analysis employed here in hypotheticals may not be sufficient for testimony or for real-world valuations.

CHAPTER 2

History and Taxonomy

Intangibles have been around a long time. The first prehistoric cave dweller who was able to start fires on purpose possessed some extremely valuable knowledge. That know-how was an intangible asset. Early agrarian societies that farmed together possessed valuable organizational capital. Their collective effort created an intangible asset. The people who created an alphabet, or a calendar, or a system of numbers were early inventors of extremely important intangible assets. If only they had been able to patent their inventions or copyright their works!

Before we go any further, we need to establish that there is nothing that precludes intangibles from being assets, at least from a definitional standpoint. Setting aside the definition that it is the property of the deceased, *Merriam-Webster's Collegiate Dictionary* defines an asset as "the entire property of a person, association, corporation, or estate applicable or subject to the payment of debts," or as an "advantage or resource" as in "his wit is his chief asset."[1] In the Original Pronouncements of the Financial Accounting Standards Board (FASB), assets are defined as "probable future economic benefits obtained or controlled by a particular entity as a result of past transactions or events."[2]

Neither the dictionary nor the accounting definition of an asset requires it to be tangible in nature. Using the example from the preface, both the pharmaceutical company's patent portfolio and the education of the college student can qualify; both result from some transaction (developing the drugs) or investment (attending the college), and they represent future economic benefit that is controlled by the drug company or the student. In the case of the student, the control is undeniable; in the case of the patents, that control could be revoked by the patent office (as is discussed below).

TYPES OF INTANGIBLE ASSETS

All firms have two kinds of assets: those we can touch and those we cannot. The kind that we can see, feel, taste, buy, sell, and so on are, of course, called tangible assets. Everything else is an intangible asset. Within intangibles, the distinction usually is made between *identifiable intangibles* and *unidentifiable intangibles*. Identifiable intangibles include *intellectual property* (IP), such as patents, copyrights, trademarks, and trade secrets, among others. Figure 2.1 depicts this basic classification of assets. The gray area represents proto-assets, which are a topic for Chapter 5.

Within the theoretical framework of this book, the distinction as to whether an intangible is identifiable or not, or intellectual property or not, is unimportant. Those are not necessarily economic distinctions. The focus of this text is on the economic benefit that can be derived and the degree of ownership or control that a firm has over the intangible asset. Although it is true that identifiable intangibles, such as intellectual property, tend to be more clearly owned or controllable, that characteristic does not necessarily translate into economic benefit. It is also not true that identification (the legal and accounting distinction) is sufficient or even necessary to place an intangible on the financial statement.

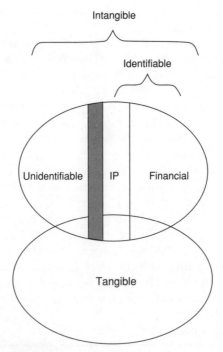

FIGURE 2.1   Assets of a Firm.

Tangible assets often have intangibles associated with them. This is why in Figure 2.1 there is overlap between a firm's tangible and intangible assets. There are patents associated with many durable goods; a car or airplane, for instance, is a virtual repository of patented technologies. The car or airplane also will carry brands, trademarks, and copyrights (e.g., on the owner's manuals). These intangibles need not be the same intangibles that the firm might develop and market independently. General Motors, for instance, has a large portfolio of intellectual property that it licenses (e.g., trademarks on older vehicles) separate and apart from the patents and trademarks in the firm's current product offerings. This is how Revell can make toy models of Corvettes. Revell licenses the right from GM. Otherwise, Revell would have to make models of a more generic Fun Car.

Figure 2.1 also shows financial assets. All financial assets are intangible, although sometimes they, too, are securitized by physical assets. Cash and cash equivalents are not real property; cash needs no valuation, and by definition cash equivalents do not need much of one. Can we imagine applying, say, the income method to value how much cash some cash will generate?

IDENTIFIABLE INTANGIBLES

This section describes many identifiable assets, including the "typical" groups, such as patents, copyrights, trademarks, and trade secrets. It also includes some intangibles that certainly can be identified (most notably, research and development), although in most instances accounting conventions would not treat them as assets.

Intellectual Property

When people think about identifiable intangible assets, intellectual property is what comes to mind most often. Intellectual property includes:

- Patents
- Copyrights
- Trademarks
- Trade secrets

One feature that intellectual property intangibles have in common is that historically they have been provided with some legal protection or recognition. The concept of a patent goes back at least as far as medieval Venetian law, and was codified by Thomas Jefferson in the United States in the 1793 Patent Act. The U.S. Copyright Act has existed since 1790. This legal characteristic—the fact that all of these intangibles are deemed "property" as a matter of law—qualifies them as intellectual property.

But legal protection for intangibles is by no means rock solid. Legal status does not guarantee that the economic benefit associated with some particular intangible asset, such as a patent, will not be revoked. The courts may support a challenge to a patent's validity, which would remove the holder's legal claim. In fact, 526 patent infringement lawsuits were filed in the United States in 2003. In 308 of them the patent was deemed invalid or unenforceable.[3]

Assets of intellectual property also often share a consequential economic characteristic of being marketable. Intellectual property frequently is sold by or bought or licensed from patent holders because it can be. Patents and copyrights in particular often are purchased or assigned to someone other than the original inventor or creator. For example, most of the Beatles' publishing catalog is now owned by Michael Jackson. In the music business, song catalogs often are sold as their expected revenue streams decline over time— hence the endless greatest hits collections offered on late-night television.

The defining accounting requirements—that intangible assets be identifiable and separable—also are directly related. Accounting rules, which we will discuss at length in Chapter 4, make this distinction, too. Intellectual property assets are separable and identifiable, and they can be bought and sold apart from whoever creates or originally owns them.

Patents

Patent Offices   Worldwide, there are more than two dozen patent offices. The United States Patent and Trademark Office or (USPTO) was officially created by the 1793 Patent Act. The European Patent Office was founded in 1977 under the European Patent Convention.[4] The Japanese Patent Office was founded in the late nineteenth century. The World Intellectual Property Organization (WIPO), created by the United Nations, also represents an international collection of patent information, largely as a result of the Patent Cooperation Treaty (PCT). The PCT is a system of registration to which many patent authorities around the world subscribe.

At their core, all of these offices serve the same purpose: to act as a registry for intellectual property. These organizations establish whether some application for an invention meets various criteria, and then record the invention as having been created and owned by the patentee. Because of many of the economic properties of intangible assets (which we discuss at length in Chapter 3), there has been enormous interest in protecting assets in foreign countries. Both the easy exchange of digital information and the digital nature of much intellectual property have made infringement and piracy increasingly attractive. Notwithstanding the importance of harmonizing international patent law, this book mostly focuses on patents in the context of the United States.

Patent Applications   The cost to obtain a patent is not nominal, nor is the application process rapid. The increase in intangibles over the last several decades has placed a significant burden on the patent office. Typically, it takes two to three years to win patent approval or rejection.[5] The application for a patent (usually crafted by a patent attorney) includes the language of the patent, the review of prior art, and assurance that the application meets other legal criteria.

Patent Criteria   Patents must be "novel, non-obvious, and useful." A purported invention is deemed nonobvious if it would not be obvious to one of ordinary skill in the relevant art. Lawyers or economists, for instance, cannot judge the nonobviousness of an invention that is used on farms, but a farmer could. The economic implications of what is nonobvious are explored throughout the book, especially in Chapters 7 and 9. If successful, patent holders now have the right to exclude others from making, using, or selling their invention for a period of 20 years from the application filing. Patents filed before June 8, 1995, have slightly different rules.

Types of Patents   There are several types of patents, including utility, design, plant, and animal. This book focuses on utility patents. A design patent essentially covers the way some element of an invention looks, usually without directly incorporating the underlying utility of the invention: "Whoever invents any new, original and ornamental design for an article of manufacture may obtain a patent therefor, subject to the conditions and requirements of this title. The provisions of this title relating to patents for inventions shall apply to patents for designs, except as otherwise provided."[6]

A utility patent covers a methodology, formula, or technology that results in the creation of a new invention: "Whoever invents or discovers any new and useful process, machine, manufacture, or composition of matter, or any new and useful improvement thereof, may obtain a patent therefor, subject to the conditions and requirements of this title."[7] This definition provides the groundwork for many lawsuits. Perhaps most interesting is the subset of utility patents that have commonly become known as process patents or method patents.

Process Patents   Process patents extend the meaning of the word "process" beyond what many legal experts feel was the original intention, which had more to do with chemical, technical, or industrial formulas. During the Internet heyday of the late 1990s, many start-up technology firms filed for process patents that described some method for purchasing or browsing that (in theory) would be useful to everyone involved in e-commerce. For example, patents were filed on the concept of a "shopping cart" and "selling digital downloads." A patent was filed on the "process" of using a modem to connect to the Internet.

One of the most famous process patents was Amazon's "1-Click" buying feature, whereby various elements of the customer's profile were combined to streamline the online purchasing process. In a controversial 1999 lawsuit Amazon filed against its largest competitor, barnesandnoble.com, Amazon claimed that upholding the validity of the 1-Click patent was important because it had invested a great deal of programming effort to develop what it considered a competitive advantage. Jeffrey Bezos, Amazon's chief executive officer, pointed out correctly that, in order to encourage innovation, it is vital to have legal protection for inventors to be able to appropriate some of the fruits of their labor. Initially, the court agreed, issuing an injunction against Barnes & Noble that prevented the firm from using its version of "1-Click." Eventually the injunction was overturned. Meanwhile, Barnes & Noble had developed its own new version of a streamlined method, which was essentially "2-Click." Although Amazon and Barnes & Noble settled out of court in 2002, the legal debate over Amazon's patent and the broader debate over method patents have not ended.[8]

Designing around a Patent   Even though many Internet-related process patents were approved, not surprisingly, few resulted in economic benefit to their inventors. This is especially true when patents purported to cover a process that was either so obvious or so easy to design around that the patent was worthless. "Design-around," "engineer-around," or "reverse-engineer" are terms used to describe when a competing inventor is able to obtain the benefits of a patented technology without infringing the patent in question. During the late 1990s, critics of the USPTO wondered whether the patent reviewers had forgotten the test of nonobviousness. In fact, during the heat of the Barnes & Noble lawsuit, the rapidly changing patent landscape even led Amazon's Bezos to wonder publicly if the life of Internet business patents should be reduced to a few years. Other observers have wondered if the length or strength of patent protection should be gauged along a scale of obviousness.

Economic Rationale   Why grant patents at all? There is a simple economic rationale: If people cannot appropriate some of the rents due to an invention, then they will have little incentive to create the invention in the first place. A patent often is described as the granting of a temporary monopoly. In reward for expending the efforts to develop a patentable idea or technology, the patent office grants the patent holder the right for some limited time to exclude others from using the invention described by the patent. On one hand this may seem at odds with antitrust laws, which at first blush seem to suggest that encouraging monopolies is not a good idea. Yet there are also broader procompetitive effects of granting the protection. Consumers of the patented good are able to benefit from its employ in the marketplace. And competitors, although excluded from using the patented technology directly, will forgo the wasteful duplication of research efforts; thus, in theory at least, creating more social benefit. It is important to remember that monopolies are oftentimes good for consumers; patent law generally supports this notion, hoping that enforced expiration of the patent creates the right balance of incentives: enough protection to encourage innovation, but not so much to encourage abuse.

Copyrights

U.S. copyright law was established in 1790; but the idea of a copyright goes back to late fifteenth-century England when the printing press was introduced. Copyrights usually are made in creative works or written material, such as books, music, photographic images, illustrations, screenplays, television and film broadcasts, and software code. Unlike with patents, the process for applying for a copyright is relatively straightforward. In fact, the creator of the work owns the copyright as soon as the work is created. Filing of a copyright registration simply gives notice that the creator is claiming a copyright in the work. Although registration is a prerequisite for an infringement lawsuit, and is beneficial in litigation with regard to burden of proof and damages, registration does not conclusively establish ownership.[9]

As an interesting aside, the person who claims a copyright need not have willfully violated some preexisting copyrighted work to be found liable (and to lose his or her own later copyright). Unlike with patents, the copyright office does not screen an applicant's submission of registration for possible violations of preexisting copyrighted material. In a famous case filed against the former Beatle George Harrison, the owners of the copyright on the 1960s pop song "He's So Fine" successfully prevailed in court, claiming that Harrison had stolen the song and used the melody in his 1971 hit, "My Sweet Lord." There is no reason to believe that Mr. Harrison willfully violated the copyright; but under copyright law, ignorance is not a defense to liability, although it may be relevant in determining damages.

Copyrights in a Digital World   With the advent of the digitalization of enormous quantities of copyrighted material over the last two decades, one of the most interesting intersections of intellectual property law and intangible assets is in the concept of *fair use*. Fair use is "any use of copyrighted material that does not infringe copyright even though it is done without the authorization of the copyright holder and without an explicit exemption from infringement under copyright law."[10] Since fair use is widely misinterpreted, some history is required.

Up until the last two decades, owners of copyrighted material, such as books, records, or film, would not often face mass copying of their works. Piracy was difficult. This situation began to change with the advent of consumer recording and videotaping technology, and the courts were forced to address these issues.

In 1984, in the *Sony v. Universal City Studios* decision, the Supreme Court held that one form of videotaping—called timeshifting—was legal and constituted fair use. Timeshifting means, for example, taping a television show for viewing once at a more convenient time.

Other litigation has extended the timeshifting concept. The outcome of a second Sony lawsuit was a settlement that resulted in the Audio Home Recording Act (AHRA) of 1992, which essentially provided safe harbor for home users. This defense has been cited in numerous copyright actions involving digital media, the most recent of which are lawsuits filed by the major motion picture studios against firms selling DVD copying software. This defense is unlikely to prevail; the AHRA did not address downloading, nor does it comprehensively address digital recording.

The 1998 Digital Millennium Copyright Act (DCMA), although still imperfect, protects copyright holders from many types of violations that could not have even been conceived in 1790. The DCMA deems circumvention of digital protection mechanisms to be illegal and also prohibits the sale or manufacture of technology "primarily designed" for the purposes of circumventing some encryption technology. It also recognizes some limitations on copyright. For instance, the act allows archiving of computer programs.

It remains to be seen how the courts will balance the rights of copyright holders with free speech and the right to individual privacy. The courts have ruled that commercial entities cannot copy digital music files for individual use, but they have not explicitly ruled whether individuals themselves may do so. There are also important economic considerations. Findings of contributory liability—which would implicate the technology that has made digital replication possible—can have a potentially harmful dampening effect on innovation that is good for society. In 2003 in the *MGM v. Grokster* case, the court cited numerous other permissive uses that for example, reduced distribution costs.[11] In other words, file-swapping software or DVD-ripping software itself can have socially valuable, procompetitive, legal uses, even if it often is used for illegal ones. There are also some privacy issues. The

Recording Industry Association of America (RIAA) was unable to invoke the DMCA's subpoena provision to learn the identities of possible infringers via Verizon Internet services.

Copyright holders struggle to find other ways to prevent unauthorized use of their digital material. One such method is digital-rights management software—tracking mechanisms that allow only certain numbers or types of copies to be made. Major movie studios in particular are concerned with this issue, since the speed and cost of replicating DVDs (either directly or via download) likely will not remain much of a stumbling block for more sophisticated pirates. To determine whether bad social or firm outcomes outweigh the good, we would have to undertake an economic analysis.

Trade Secrets

Trade secrets are types of assets that result from a proprietary technology or way of doing business. Generally speaking, they exist because they provide some competitive advantage. They are not merely one-time secrets, such as how much a particular customer was willing to pay on a given invoice, but rather something that is used in the ongoing business, like a unique accounting system or a closely guarded formula. Trade secrets have their legal origins in two different sources, the Uniform Trade Secret Act (UTSA) of 1985 and the Restatement (First) of Torts of 1939. (The latter will be discussed in Chapter 9.) According to UTSA: "'Trade secret' means information, including a formula, pattern, compilation, program, device, method, technique, or process, that: (i) derives independent economic value, actual or potential, from not being generally known to, and not being readily ascertainable by proper means by, other persons who can obtain economic value from its disclosure or use, and (ii) is the subject of efforts that are reasonable under the circumstances to maintain its secrecy."[12] A customer list, a recipe, and a factory floor layout all might qualify as trade secrets, provided that there is value in the fact they remain unknown to the competition—that is, that they provide independent economic value, and that there is some evidence that their owners actually try to keep them secret.

Whereas two firms cannot own two separate patents on the same exact invention, it is possible for two firms to independently and simultaneously hold the same information as a trade secret. In other words, owning a trade secret does not foreclose the perfectly legal possibility that someone else also considers the same information theirs. It is less likely that these firms compete directly, though, because if they do, their ability to derive "independent economic value" is probably limited—competition eats the advantage away.

Trade Secrets versus Patents   Trade secrets are different from patents in three ways.

1. Trade secrets cover more territory than patents. Not all trade secrets can be patented.
2. Trade secrets are not predicated on their providing usefulness to society.
3. Unlike patents, trade secrets do not require nonobviousness or novelty.

As discussed, inventors are granted patents as rewards to spur the creation of useful ideas for society. Trade secrets are given some legal protection simply to prevent theft from their owners. Others may discover the secret by legitimate means (say, reverse-engineering) and can then use it themselves. For example, a company may be able to exploit an improved process for manufacturing an automobile tire without disclosing that process (and thus retain that process as a trade secret), but an improved tire tread design becomes publicly known as soon as the first tire with that tread is sold (making trade secret protection for that design essentially impossible).

What makes inventors decide to patent their inventions, rather than retain them as trade secrets? According to law and economics scholars David Friedman, William Landes, and Richard Posner, when firms make this decision, trade secret law (which is largely common law) supplements federal patent law: "Inventors choose trade secret protection when they believe that patent protection is too costly relative to the value of their invention, or that it [patent protection] will give them a reward substantially less than the benefit of their invention."[13]

The second clause is the more important one. Although patents grant the owner a monopoly, patents also make inventions public. Therefore, if the owners of an invention want to patent it, they have to consider the risk that the benefit of protection outweighs the benefit of secrecy. If they decide to patent (and publish) their invention, they may be providing a road map for competitors to design around the patent. Remember, reverse-engineering a trade secret is perfectly legal; only stealing it is not. Depending on the strength of the patent itself—which is measured both by the legal interpretation and by the uniqueness of the invention—keeping a trade secret secret may be the right economic decision.

Recently the ability to keep secrets has been impacted by efforts to harmonize with European conventions. One of these efforts is a movement to require pregrant publication and public review of the prior art on a patent application.[14]

Figure 2.2 depicts the patent–trade secret decision along two dimensions: the incentive to patent and the benefit of secrecy. The greater the ben-

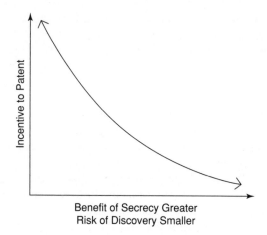

Benefit of Secrecy Greater
Risk of Discovery Smaller

FIGURE 2.2   Trade Secret or Patent.

efit of keeping the invention secret—say because a patent would provide a design-around road map—the lower the incentive to patent. If there is little benefit of keeping the invention secret—for example, if there is a high risk of discovery or a high risk that a legal claim of ownership of the trade secret will fail (with little evidence that the owner took any steps to maintain secrecy)—then the incentive to patent is greater.

Trademarks

Like copyrights, trademarks can be established through common-law usage, although there are legal advantages to registration. Trademarks are registered with the United States Patent and Trademark Office in a process that is somewhere between the patent and copyright processes in terms of the legal assistance required and the amount of review conducted.

Trademark Confusion   Although a trademark search is not necessary, usually an attorney conducts one to determine what other trademarks exist (senior marks) that could be confused with the one under consideration (junior mark). There is some economic analysis involved at this stage. Two firms might hold very similar trademarks, but if they are not likely to be confused, both trademarks might be able to coexist. Trademarks are granted for use with particular classes of goods; service marks are granted for use with particular classes of services. "Box-Mate" might be a kitty litter box accessory; "Boxmate" might be a tool used for fabricating corrugated cardboard boxes. These are in entirely different product classes, and their similarity is not likely to cause confusion.

A common area of inquiry is whether trademarks potentially overlap customer geographies. Trademark protection is national and often can be international. Through the Madrid system, WIPO registers thousands of international trademarks annually. Because a dozen or more countries subscribe to the WIPO system, cross registration translates into millions of national trademarks worldwide. With increasing sales and advertising via the Internet, even in the United States, the traditional geographical definition is not always adequate.

Trademark Dilution Suppose there is a single-location hair salon in Phoenix called George's. It is not likely to be confused with one in Chicago by the same name based on geography alone. But consider whether customers from one city frequently travel to the other city. And consider whether George's in Chicago sells its own brand of hair-care products on several online Web sites. If these circumstances are true, there well may be the potential for trademark and/or service mark confusion. If things got bad enough, the owners of the George's in Chicago might consider filing a lawsuit against the store in Phoenix based on the theory of *trademark dilution*—the idea that the Phoenix salon's use of the name is hurting the Chicago salon's business. Trademark dilution was recently heard before the Supreme Court. In the 2003 case, *Moseley et al., dba Victor's Little Secret v. V Secret Catalogue, Inc., et al.*, the Court came down firmly in requiring that actual dilution, and not the likelihood of it, needed to be established. (We will discuss this at more length in Chapter 9.)

To use a mark that is similar to an existing trademark is not per se illegal. Sometimes it even makes sense to forgo registering a mark, because such registration puts the holder of the mark on notice that the applicant exists.

Trade Dress Trade dress is another related concept. It usually refers to features of packaging in which the trademark owner claims a property right. Color is a good example of trade dress. Think of the unique brown and orange color of packages of Reese's peanut butter cups or the robin's egg blue of a Tiffany box. It is easy to imagine lawsuits that would arise if their competitors imitated such trade dress. It is not surprising that packaging properties are intangible assets. Although color formulas often are patented, color palettes themselves are important pieces of intellectual property for paint companies. The formulas that create different hues, tones, and shades of color require substantial research. Sometimes their owners register the names of colors and collections of colors. In fact, the ability to reproduce color accurately gave birth to the Pantone company, which created a language for "color communication."

Fonts also are elements of a tradedress. Think of the Coca-Cola name without its famous cursive writing. Coca-Cola certainly does not own cursive, and it probably could not prevent a company from writing in a similar style—unless that writing was included as part of a mark that competes with Coke products or somehow could be construed as diluting Coca-Cola's mark. Font-making used to be a bigger business before scalable fonts were made part of most word-processing programs, typesetters had to buy custom fonts and font libraries from software designers who specialized in digital typesetting.

Research and Development

As we will see in Chapters 3 and 4, research and development (R&D) expense recorded by public firms has been the topic of a great deal of academic research, largely because, historically, R&D expense was one of only two intangible items routinely reported in public company financial statements; the other was goodwill.

R&D is sometimes an identifiable intangible asset because it can directly result in intellectual property—a firm's research can turn into patents, which, in turn, may be bought and sold separately. Although a large component of the expenditures on R&D never materialize in patents, this fact does not mean that the firm gets nothing in return; marketable patents are not the end goal for many R&D investments. Often firms invent and improve manufacturing techniques, software codes, and trade secrets without any intention of patenting them. And often firms apply for patents without any intention of marketing the assets covered by those patents.

Brands

Trademarks, copyrights, patents, and even harder-to-classify intangibles all converge in brands. There is no simple definition of what a brand is, but at the center is the concept that it is an economic asset, not just a way to label a product. Brands are much more than simply names or trademarks. Tom Blackett of Interbrand, a famous brand consulting firm, writes about brands as business assets:

> *Brands that keep their promise attract loyal buyers who will return to them at regular intervals. The benefit to the brand owner is that fore-casting cash flows becomes easier, and it becomes possible to plan and manage the development of the business with greater confidence. Thus,*

brands, with their ability to secure income, can be classed as productive assets in exactly the same way as any other, more traditional assets of a business (plant, equipment, cash, investments, and so on).[15]

Economic Benefit Brands add value because they convey information about a product. For example, consumers may associate durability with a particular brand of jeans, and they may be willing to pay more for durability. While it is true that in the short run the pants maker could cut corners and make even more money by trading on its good name, eventually the market will discover the fraud and consumers would be unwilling to pay a premium for the brand. For this reason, brand owners have the incentive to "keep their promise."

Naming Rights Naming rights are an important extension of a firm's brand. Two of the most interesting extensions are domain names and building names. Companies like to have an Internet address associated with their company name, although how much a particular domain name creates value is not yet clearly established. Looking at the bygone days of dot-com euphoria, researchers Michael Cooper, Orlin Dimitrov, and P. Raghavendra Rau found a "striking positive stock price reaction to the announcement of corporate name changes to Internet-related dotcom names." But while the positive effect on stock price apparently was not transitory, it also was not associated with how much Internet business the firms really did.[16]

A more important reason to secure rights to similar Uniform Resource Locators (URLs) is motivated by a company's concern that inappropriate use of the most obvious one or two Web site addresses similar to its own would have a detrimental effect on its brand. For a limited time over the last decade, cyber-squatters made a living from registering the likely domain names of large, popular companies and then selling them back to the firms. The courts have largely tended to favor the firms in such cases, since the very purpose of registering those names was to hold the established users for ransom.

A less defensive use of naming rights comes in the form of building names and, in particular, the names of sports arenas. In 1988 there were just three naming-rights deals with a total contract value of $25 million. By 2004 there were 66 deals worth $3.6 billion.[17] Although these investments usually are mentioned as a marketing expense, these intangibles have not been included on balance sheets, probably because the causal connection to value is still unclear.

We return to brands in Chapter 5, where we discuss how brand experts go about placing a value on what is really a collection of many intangibles.

Software Code

Software code is arguably the most complicated intellectual property to codify, because it is possible to copyright the code, patent the business process that the code enables, keep part of the code as a trade secret, and trademark features of the software design. Firms make intense (in percentage terms, usually dominating) investments in intellectual capital to develop a piece of software. And the way firms eventually use and sell software code can reflect different accounting treatment. This treatment largely depends on whether software is an input to manufacturing a firm's good or whether the software is the firm's good, and how proprietary the software investment is.

For example, most law firms have a significant amount of money tied up in the software that they use. Firms might run Microsoft Office for word processing and spreadsheet calculations; Intuit's QuickBooks for the firm's bookkeeping; and Thomson's Westlaw for online research. None of these investments, however, would qualify as valuable intangible property. There is nothing proprietary to the law firm's use of Office, QuickBooks, and Westlaw. Virtually all law firms use the same or similar programs, and having them cannot really be considered some form of competitive advantage, because their use by one firm does not provide an incremental economic benefit over that firm's competitors. Nevertheless, Office, QuickBooks, and Westlaw are extremely valuable intangible property to their creators: Microsoft, Intuit, and Thomson. The purpose for which a particular piece of software is developed determines its accounting treatment. (We will expand on this in Chapter 4).

UNIDENTIFIABLE INTANGIBLE ASSETS

No less important than identifiable assets, unidentifiable intangibles are firm assets that remain hidden, at least in an accounting sense, until some transaction (i.e., an acquisition) gives rise to their identification. Goodwill is the most commonly discussed unidentifiable. It usually is created as the result of firm-specific capital.

Goodwill

Goodwill has a very specific accounting meaning, which does not simply reflect some accumulation of customer loyalty or satisfaction, repeat business, or good relationships. Those are the *result of* other assets, tangible or intangible. Customers come back because the products are superior, or the service is better, not because of goodwill. Goodwill, as defined by financial accountants, is a residual, created when one firm buys another firm for more than the fair value of the net identifiable assets, both tangible and intangible.

Although there are other unidentifiable intangibles, conventional accounting rules do not provide much insight into measuring them. An example of such an intangible might be an efficiently organized factory floor. Imagine that the floor organizational plan saves a firm 5 percent more in manufacturing costs than any other comparable firm. If the efficient organizational plan can be patented, then, of course, it is no longer unidentifiable. But often that efficiency lies unspecified; management may be unable to pinpoint the reasons for its cost savings. Or, alternatively, management may know the exact reasons but may wish to keep it a trade secret. Should the managers sell the firm, however, the value of the plan for factory floor efficiency can wind up as a component of goodwill.

Although customer lists are identifiable, frequently they are cited as intangibles that contribute to an excess of fair market value being paid in an acquisition. In other words, customer lists generate goodwill. But for us to correctly ascribe value to a customer list, we must be precise about exactly how the customer list adds value.

It could be that the form of the list itself (perhaps in an electronic database) is a valuable piece of information. For a company with many customers, accurate information on their location, whom to contact, or the models of products the customers have bought is itself valuable. Warranty business is a case where accurately identifying customers is important. The organization of the customer information is costly, so a database is valuable. Customer lists also can represent cost savings if the process of identifying customers itself is costly in terms of marketing and sales effort.

Alternatively, customer lists often are viewed as stand-ins for the long-term expected sales revenue that existing and prospective customers will generate. In this case, the lists are believed to represent repeat business or promising leads. If existing customers are locked in to long-term purchasing agreements, then interpreting the customer list as a valuable (identifiable) intangible makes some sense. But in the long run, repeat business from existing customers or new business is going to result from desirable product attributes or other services the company delivers. Those features may be the unidentifiable intangibles that we wish to measure. In this view, a customer list does not mean much; rather, a desirable product offering is more likely to be the source of secure future revenues.

Human Capital

Before University of Chicago economist and Nobel Prize–winner Gary Becker published a book entitled *Human Capital* in 1964, the term was not part of the ordinary business lexicon. Becker (along with Sherwin Rosen,

Milton Friedman, Jacob Mincer, and Ted Schultz) established the economic concept of human capital as distinct from financial or physical assets, because, unlike those assets, human capital cannot be separated from the humans who possess it. He writes:

> *Schooling, a computer training course, expenditures on medical care, and lectures on the virtues of punctuality and honesty are capital too in the sense that they improve health, raise earnings, or add to a person's appreciation of literature over much of his or her lifetime. Consequently, it is fully in keeping with the capital concept as traditionally defined to say that expenditures on education, training, medical care, etc., are all investments in capital.*[18]

Not too long after Becker firmed up the concept of human capital, economists and consultants began to subdivide and classify types of human capital. Without limitation, it means both physical and intellectual ability. The terms "intellectual capital," "organizational capital," and "knowledge capital" frequently are used interchangeably and incorrectly. There is no meaningful distinction between intellectual capital and knowledge capital. Both can belong to a firm or an individual. The term "knowledge capital" may have gained currency primarily as a marketing tool in connection with a discipline called knowledge management. For simplicity, we use the term "intellectual capital" throughout.

But the term "organizational capital" implicitly means capital that resides within an organization. And we must further distinguish who owns it within the organization. Some organizational capital comes about as a result of the specific arrangement of assets of a firm; other organizational capital simply resides within the firm, such as the educations of the employees.

This book does not consider the latter to be organizational capital—it is "ordinary" intellectual capital. The firm gets to make use of its employees' education, but the firm does not own the employees. Here we call firm-specific creations *organizational capital*. This kind of capital stays at the firm even when the workers go home at the end of the day. For example, an efficiency-creating assembly-floor layout, or a firm's collected product knowledge base or list of frequently asked questions (FAQs) live on even when the employees who created them are no longer at the firm. And if that capital is codified in patents or copyrights or trade secrets, it then is no longer unidentifiable.

Another form of organizational capital is more temporal: It is the shared knowledge or efficiencies that result from particular employees working together. Take, for instance, an attorney and her legal assistant who have worked together for many years. The way that they get work done together may be highly efficient, and, as a result, it creates economic benefits for the firm. Yet neither can take those efficiencies home with her at night, nor can the firm keep the benefits without keeping the team together. Other scenarios can be imagined—where the team shares their methods with the rest of the firm, or where the two decide to write a management book—but for our purposes, what is important is to recognize that "gray area" organizational capital exists. It is one of the most difficult topics for valuation; these assets are generally hidden and difficult to assess in terms of ownership.

LIABILITIES

So far the discussion has revolved entirely around intangible assets. Do intangible liabilities exist? One way to answer this is to ask another question: Are there *tangible* liabilities?[19] By definition, most liabilities are contractual, and all are intangible. They are created primarily as a way to delay payment for something, usually an asset or an expense, such as labor or sales and marketing. As the Original Pronouncements of the Financial Accounting Standards Board make clear: "Liabilities are claims of creditors against the enterprise, arising out of past activities, that are to be satisfied by the disbursement or utilization of corporate resources."[20] We do not need to talk about intangible liabilities, because in the valuation context, assets and liabilities are a net proposition. In case readers are not convinced, let us work through an example.

Financial (Intangible) Liabilities

Assume for the example that a hypothetical firm Test Company has a low-interest revolving credit facility. Suppose that Test Company's owners have negotiated the debt to allow them to borrow at 5 percent, while all of Test Company's competition borrows at 8 percent. If regular draws on this credit facility are important to success in the business, is not their 3 percent edge an intangible liability?

The answer depends on *why* Test Company's owners were able to achieve a more favorable rate than their competitors. If Test Company really is identical to its competitors in all important ways—management quality, product success, manufacturing facilities, and the like—then it could be the case that Test Company was just lucky, and in the right place at the right time. Perhaps the bank needed to make some uneconomic loans for its own reasons.

More probable, though, is that some other asset distinguishes Test Company from the rest of the field. In fact, the more that Test Company appears on the surface to look like the competition, the more likely that its superior credit revolver is the result of some intangible asset. After reviewing Test Company's financial information, the bank may have been swayed by a superior management team, or better prospects for product expansion, or a state-of-the-art manufacturing facilities. Even some luck might be explained this way. Test Company's management may have a knack for being in the right place at the right time to negotiate favorable loans. With everything else constant, differences in the cost of capital should reflect underlying differences in the economic prospects of companies—that is, their creditors anticipate that the arrangement of assets at one firm is likely to produce more return than the arrangement at the others.

Provisions for Risk

Not all intangible liabilities are financial instruments. Suppose that we are interested in valuing a manufacturing facility located near a river. Let us further assume that once every so often the river overflows its banks, ruining whatever inventory was on the loading docks. This propensity for the river to ruin Test Company's inventory periodically is, of course, not an asset. But it is also not unforeseen, at least in the way we have assumed that things happen. Indeed, a good valuation—and a good accounting statement—will make provisions for this contingency. The amount for which the company should provision, or the amount for which we should reduce our valuation of Test Company, might be equal (as a first approximation) to the probability of the river overflowing, multiplied by the value of the lost inventory. Some more details go into that calculation of the probability (e.g., is flooding more likely with each successive year, or is each year independent?), but this type of calculation and provisioning for losses is done every day under the rubric of risk management. The provision for river losses is directly offset by the expected decrease in the value of the inventory account—which is, in this case, a tangible asset. In other words, intangible liabilities exist, but they really can be explained as a decrease in value of some asset with which they are associated.

WHAT IS NOT AN INTANGIBLE ASSET

A few economic concepts that are not intangible assets are worth mentioning:

- Competitive advantage
- Market share
- Added value
- Efficiency
- Repeat business
- Customer loyalty

As made clear from the example of the company that has access to cheaper debt, it is important to separate the result of intangibles from the underlying economic engine that creates the result. One firm cannot sell its "competitive advantage" to another firm, but it might license its manufacturing know-how or patents that result in competitive advantage. Similarly, firms do not buy "market share"; firms acquire products or competitors whose products constitute a share of the market. "Efficiency" is another good example. It is the result of better work processes or of trade secrets; it is not a stand-alone asset.

SUMMARY

This chapter presented many of the terms used to describe intangibles. We made the distinction between identifiable and unidentifiable intangibles, and, under those classifications, discussed various forms of intellectual property and knowledge capital. We also discussed some of the economic and legal issues surrounding patents, copyrights, and trademarks, three of the more commercialized forms of intangibles. We also explained how goodwill is created by some underlying economic assets.

ADDITIONAL RESOURCES

A number of Web sites provide useful additional reference information. Readers interested in patents should first visit the USPTO Web site at www.uspto.gov, and the World Intellectual Property Organization (WIPO) site at www.wipo.org. WIPO has several global protection systems in addition to the Patent Cooperation Treaty (PCT) system for patents mentioned earlier. WIPO also registers international trademarks through the Madrid system and catalogs industrial designs through the Hague system.

Readers interested in copyright information should visit the U.S. Copyright Office's Web site at www.copyright.gov as well as the Office for Harmonization in the Internal Market at www.oami.eu.int/en. The Berne Convention Treaty provides some historical perspective about international copyrights; its text can be found at www.law.cornell.edu/treaties/berne/overview.html. Statutes on patents, copyrights, and trademarks can all be found at the U.S. Government Printing Office site, www.access.gpo.gov.

The site for the American Intellectual Property Law Association is www.aipla.org, and the Intellectual Property Owners site is www.ipo.org.

A useful patent search tool is found through the IBM Intellectual Property Network at www.ibm.com/ibm/licensing/.

CHAPTER 3

Theory of and Research on Intangible Assets

This chapter is in some ways the rationale for picking up this book—namely, that the theory of and research on intangible assets tells us there is value in the things we cannot touch. That fact may seem obvious, but proving it is not so easy. The peculiar characteristics of intangible assets have spawned research from a wide range of academics, especially accountants and economists. In this chapter we explore some economic characteristics of intangible assets. Also, we examine data trends in their prevalence, as well as research that ties those intangible assets to a measure of value. Keep in mind that our examination of the literature is selective only. The references section at the end of the book provides additional reading.

SOME ECONOMIC CHARACTERISTICS OF INTANGIBLES

This section describes some of the economic characteristics of intangible assets. These characteristics include low marginal cost coupled with frequently high initial costs, economies of scale, joint consumption, imperfect substitution, and sometimes network effects.

Low Marginal Cost

Intangible assets exhibit some powerful traits that their tangible cousins do not always share. The first trait is that intangible assets are often *scalable*. Put slightly differently, this means that it costs little either to duplicate the asset itself or to duplicate the economic benefits that can be derived from the asset. An economist would describe the production of such an asset as one with very low marginal cost. In extreme cases (which is often so with intangibles), the cost to produce one more copy of the asset may even approach zero.

Take, for example, the copyright on a song. Copyright holders can make as many copies as they want without having to incur the initial creative investment all over again. This does not mean that the cost of delivering the asset to the market is zero. To be sure, acetate, vinyl, recording tape, CD-Rs, blank compact discs, or hard disk space have all at various times made mass copying prohibitively costly. Similarly, a book publisher incurs nontrivial production and distribution costs to produce an extra copy of a book, but the author does not need to write it from scratch again; that investment already has been made. In the case of software, support costs can be massive, obscuring what otherwise might seem to be a zero marginal-cost proposition. The same can be said about the marketing efforts behind a new motion picture or new drug therapy. Nonetheless, with each successive copy, the cost of creating the raw material itself—the notes in the song, the words on the page, or the code in the software—does not repeat.

In fact, this feature is at the heart of modern piracy as the digitalization of many forms of intellectual property has exploded. Consider the would-be pirate's cost to steal a song and sell bootleg copies in the days before the Internet, mp3s, cheap hard disk space, and CD burners. Without access to the original master recording, it would be difficult for a pirate to produce anything that sounded remotely as good as the original. This quality difference would limit the amount that less scrupulous (or aware) buyers would be willing to pay. Today the luxury of at least some limited protection due to technological constraints is basically nonexistent. Some estimates for 2003 find one-third of all compact discs sold worldwide are pirated copies.[1] Songs that are digitally recorded and then digitally distributed are mass-copied, illegally or legally, with near perfection; only the artwork or other limited features of the original compact disk may not be reproduced well (or at all) in the copy.

Interestingly, the ability to pirate with perfection can in some circumstances actually benefit the owner of intellectual property. When a software firm, for instance, is interested in rapidly establishing its product in the marketplace, a strategy of allowing pirated copies to circulate can help promote adoption and lock-in. The trick, of course, is to be able to control the piracy.[2]

High Initial Investment

Another characteristic that most intangibles share is high first-copy costs. Consider the enormous sums that drug companies invest in their product pipeline before commercialization is even a remote possibility. Similarly, software firms often spend many person-hours working on new product releases. Even simple-sounding programming features, such as the code that allows one to make an online purchase with a credit card, can take upward of several thousand hours of testing. Movie and television studios similarly share this investment profile. Although *Titanic* grossed over $1.8 billion and *Harry Potter and the Sorcerer's Stone* grossed nearly $1 billion, the average gross revenue for films released in 2003 was only $42 million.[3] The average cost to make a movie was nearly $103 million.[4]

Sometimes we hear that a great song or invention was created in the shower in five minutes. How can that cost the songwriter or inventor very much? Usually forgotten is the years of low pay or costly experiments in unsuccessful inventions or creations. In other words, the true cost of that "five-minute hit" includes all the hours that never paid off. Pharmaceutical firms, movie studios, software developers, and even songwriters all think of the intangible assets they create in the context of a portfolio, with the infrequent big winners subsidizing the more frequent small losers.

Economies of Scale

Related to the concepts of high initial investment and low or declining subsequent costs is the idea that intangible assets often lend themselves to supply-side *economies of scale*. This phrase means that the more of some item we wish to produce, the less it costs us on a per-item basis. Think of this as a little like producing in bulk. Once we build a factory, for example, to burn 1 million copies of the Jeff Operating System, and we have hired a sales force to sell the new product, and we have contracted for a large supply of digital media storage devices, it costs us little more to make an additional 1, 1,000, or 10,000 copies. Put another way, things get cheaper per unit the more of them we make.

Of course, goods that are custom-made can exhibit some economies of scale—for example, the custom woodworker who builds six chairs rather than five might incur little additional cost in the form of raw materials. But labor costs are unlikely to drop in terms of the cost per unit of handmade chair at anywhere near the rate of the songwriter's or software programmer's efforts to make an additional copy of the song or software. This fact occurs largely because the woodworker has little ability to scale the requisite labor input.

If, however, the woodworker decided to patent certain design elements and license that intellectual property to large furniture concerns, *that* intangible asset would be scalable; it could be used in the production of many chairs without the woodworker having to physically make each one. Of course, this means the chairs will no longer be custom made (which may or may not be a good thing, from the perspective of both the woodworker and the customers).

Joint Consumption

The woodworker who licenses design elements benefits from the fact that the intangible can be jointly consumed by more than one person at a time. That is one feature of the scalability of the intangible; another is a critical temporal quality: Many furniture makers as well as many consumers can derive benefits from the asset at exactly the same time. A more common example would be a musical concert or sports event. The Chicago Bears franchise benefits from its ability to play games in front of thousands of spectators in the stadium and millions of viewers on television at one time. Indeed, most sports teams give exactly this justification for wanting to expand their stadiums; they are going to open the doors on Sunday anyway, so why not build some extra seats?

Imperfect Substitution

Along with the technology of joint consumption, imperfect substitution is, according to University of Chicago economist Sherwin Rosen, one of the common elements that explain the economics of superstars. Superstar musicians, scientists, and athletes possess valuable intangible assets in the form of their human capital. Rosen reminds us, "[H]earing a succession of mediocre singers does not add up to a single outstanding performance. If a surgeon is 10 percent more successful in saving lives than his fellows, most people would be willing to pay more than a 10 percent premium for his services. A company involved in a $30 million law suit is rash to scrimp on the legal talent it engages." Taking the two features of superstar intangibles together, Rosen writes: "When the joint consumption technology and imperfect substitution features of preferences are combined, the possibility for talented persons to command both very large markets and very large incomes is apparent."[5]

Network Effects

Intangible assets often are at the heart of industries that depend on standards. The configurations for microprocessors, telephone and fax technology, music and video formats, and word and spreadsheet processing are all largely defined by the intellectual property in various patents and copyrights. Although it is true that these industries benefit from the scale economies just discussed, another effect sometimes is at work: Network effects result when the value of an asset increases with the number of other people who also own the asset. A phone is more useful when each neighbor also acquires a phone. My word processing program is more valuable to me when others use the same word processing program. This is sometimes described as a "positive feedback loop." But, network effects are not always positive. For example, sometimes they cause congestion: There are negative effects (in terms of access speed) for existing users when each additional user joins a high-speed cable Internet broadband service.

Whereas economies of scale occur on the supply side, network effects are driven by demand. I might benefit from more people owning telephones (in the form of a lower price) because the phone maker can achieve some scale economies. But the utility I derive from being able to synchronize with other telephones is a benefit that is separate from any cost savings I might experience. When network effects are present—that is, when benefits arise from synchronizing with other users—we should look to see if intangible assets play some role in the technical "handshake" that is required. In fact, it is most likely that a narrower category of intellectual property (patents and copyrights in particular) is involved, because publishing the standard would likely negate the possibility of trade secrets. Many standards are achieved, of course, without the coordination or ownership of commercial entities. The underlying intellectual property for these standards either is in the public domain, or the interested parties have decided to coordinate through a standard-setting body.

GROWTH IN INTANGIBLE ASSETS

The growth in intangibles has been enormous over the last few decades, across the entire spectrum of firms. Companies exist now almost entirely on intangibles, and other smokestack firms have also increased their intangibles. Human capital, too, has swelled. Let us look at some examples.

$1 Trillion Per Year

According to the work of economist Leonard Nakamura, the United States invests at least $1 trillion per year in intangibles.[6] Nakamura derives this figure by extrapolating from the fact that some 6 to 10 percent of gross domestic product (GDP) is spent on intangibles. These enormous amounts are particularly impressive because Nakamura's results are so robust. He estimates the investment using three different methodologies:

1. Corporate investment in research and development (R&D), software, and advertising
2. The salaries paid to "creative" workers (defined by Nakamura as engineers, writers, scientists, and artists)
3. Information based on operating margins

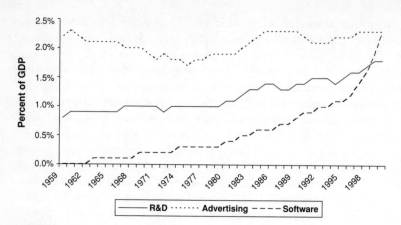

FIGURE 3.1 Research and Development, Software, and Advertising as a Percentage of GDP
Sources: Leonard Nakamura, "What Is the U.S. Gross Investment in Intangibles? (At Least) One Trillion Dollars a Year," Working Paper No. 01-15. Federal Reserve Bank of Philadelphia (October 2001).
Flow of Funds U.S. NIPA, National Science Foundation, and McCann-Erickson.

Figure 3.1 shows the percentage of GDP represented by R&D, software, and advertising. Investment in R&D and software in particular has climbed significantly in the last 40 years. And advertising spending, although perhaps not as dramatic, certainly has included a greater emphasis on brand building over simple media maintenance.

Another calculation is based on the fact that payroll for "creative" workers is about 10 percent of wages and salaries. Nakamura figures that such workers probably must then account for at least 10 percent of output—possibly an underestimate because uncounted knowledge workers, such as doctors, lawyers, and teachers, also perform creative work.

Last, there is the fact that the cost of goods sold (raw materials and the like) as a percentage of revenues has fallen by about 10 percent since 1980. This change represents a shift toward more likely intangible investments, such as R&D and advertising. Part of the increase in intangible investments comes from the movement toward counting services as intangibles: Services have increased from 22 percent of GDP in 1950 to 39 percent in 1999.[7]

New Economy and Old Economy Firms

Whole firms have been created on the basis of the economic properties of intangibles. And many old-tech or just plain old-fashioned firms have incorporated more intangible assets into their business models and have started reporting them in increasing detail.

A New Kind of Firm eBay, the dominant online auction company, is almost entirely made up of intangible assets. According to eBay's balance sheet for year-end 2003, property and equipment (physical assets) represent about 10 percent of total assets. Goodwill and intangible assets comprise about 34 percent. (Most of the remainder is cash.) Customer lists make up the overwhelming majority of intangibles, followed by trademark and trade names and, to a lesser extent, developed technologies.[8]

Figure 3.2 shows the market capitalization of software firms on the Nasdaq at the end of 2003. Microsoft and Intel alone comprise more than 10 percent of the total market capitalization of the Nasdaq.

Old-Tech Firm Even a technology giant such as IBM, legendary for its sophisticated hardware, has become more of a purveyor of intangibles. A comparison of IBM's segment revenues from 1991 to 2003 shows an enormous increase in services revenue. Services skyrocketed from less than 9 percent in 1991 to nearly 48 percent in 2003. Although the percentage for software stayed about the same (at 16 percent), revenues increased from $10.5 billion in 1991 to $14.3 billion in 2003. Meanwhile, hardware revenue plummeted from 57 percent of sales to 32 percent.[9]

Smokestack Intangibles Intangible assets also have become more visible at many traditional manufacturing firms, largely as a result of reporting

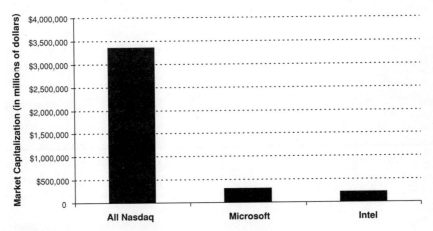

FIGURE 3.2 Market Capitalization, Year-End 2003.

TABLE 3.1   Sherwin-Williams 2000 Goodwill and Intangibles (Reported 2002)

Goodwill	Paint Stores	Consumer	Automotive Finishes	International Coatings	Consolidated Totals
Balance at January 1, 2000	$51,499	$829,632	$51,707	$106,717	$1,039,555
Acquisitions	33,417		6,763	4,638	44,818
Impairment charged to operations		(342,522)			(342,522)
Amortization	(3,494)	(23,339)	(1,820)	(3,426)	(32,079)
Currency and other adjustments	(290)	(8)	(790)	(3,137)	(4,225)
Balance at December 31, 2000	$81,132	$463,763	$55,860	$104,792	$705,547

Intangible assets subject to amortization

December 31, 2002	Software	All Other	Subtotal	Trademarks with Indefinite Lives	Total Intangible Assets
Gross	$57,802	$117,941	$175,743	$270,464	$446,207
Accumulated amortization	(6,496)	(96,725)	(103,221)	(32,594)	(135,815)
Net Value	$51,306	$21,216	$72,522	237,870	$310,392

Source: Sherwin-Williams' 2002 Annual Report.

changes in accounting based on generally accepted accounting principles (GAAP). Although this topic is covered in Chapter 4, as a preview, here we compare data in the paint company Sherwin-Williams' annual report for 2000 and 2002. In 2000, $342.5 million of goodwill was written off in the consumer segment. In 2002, goodwill was allocated to all divisions. In 2000, the company does not present how much trademarks and software were each worth. In 2002, the amount is known explicitly. Table 3.1 shows the detail given after the changes in accounting rule took place.

Another reason for the growth in intangibles at smokestack firms is that many of those companies have started to license patents, copyrights, and trademarks that often were developed as an offshoot of their primary business. In fact, even when the old business is gone, a company might live on through licensing. For example, Cragar was famous in the 1960s and 1970s as an aftermarket wheel manufacturer. Cragar mags were so popular that they became a sought-after upgrade on hot rod muscle cars. Today Cragar no longer makes wheels, but the firm licenses the name to many other wheel and toy manufacturers.

Tobin's *q* Another useful way to think about the quantity and value of intangible assets is to relate the long-run market equilibrium value of a firm to the replacement cost of the firm's assets. When these are not equivalent— that is, when the ratio is not 1—we know that the market places some value on the firm's intangibles. The larger this ratio—called Tobin's *q* after the economist James Tobin—the more the market value is explained by intangibles.[10] Figure 3.3 demonstrates an approximation of *q* for a sample of firms in 2003.[11] The formula is:

$$q = (MVE + PS + \text{DEBT}) / TA$$

where: MVE = market value of equity (closing price of shares multiplied by the common shares outstanding)
   PS = book value of outstanding preferred stock
   DEBT = short-term liabilities less short-term assets, plus book value of long-term debt
   TA = the book value of total assets

It is easy to see how different this ratio is for Internet technology firms, such as Amazon (about 10) or eBay (about 7), compared to a manufacturing firm, such as United States Steel, with a *q* ratio of well under 1. Interestingly, Dell Computer (which is essentially a manufacturing firm) exhibits a *q* ratio of around 4. Dell's success has been the subject of many analysts' scrutiny. It is likely due to the firm's emphasis on proprietary just-in-time manufacturing processes (another way of saying that there are intangible

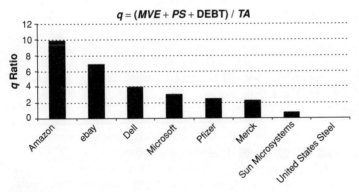

FIGURE 3.3   Approximation for Tobin's *q*, 2003
Sources: SEC Form 10-Ks.

assets at work on the factory floor) and no doubt in part due to the scale economies associated with production opportunities in an industry with enormous network effects. In other words, Dell benefits from the positive feedback loop described earlier. The utility from owning a computer increases the more people have computers. The more people have computers, the lower the prices for complementary inputs—hard drives, screens, printers, memory, and the like.

We also can look at how the q ratio has changed over time, especially for firms rich in intangibles. Figure 3.4, on the following page, compares Amazon and Microsoft over the last decade to United States Steel. The technology firms had particularly high q ratios during the rapid period of Internet expansion in the late 1990s. Even though some of the bloom came off the technology markets in 2000, those ratios still remain relatively high, especially compared to United States Steel.

Intellectual Capital

Intellectual capital, as measured by education and on-the-job training, also has grown. The fraction of 21- to 25-year-olds with some college education has nearly doubled from about 27 percent to 48 percent over the period 1963 to 1997. The work of economists Kevin M. Murphy and Finis Welch also shows that there has been greater employment growth in industries that are more education-intensive.[12]

On-the-job training has always been a significant investment. According to economist Jacob Mincer, on-the-job training (including opportunity costs) accounted for about $150 billion in 1976 (in 1987 dollars) and $200 billion in 1987—nearly half as much as the investment in schooling.[13] Although overall spending on corporate training is expected to drop, that fact does not mean less in training. On the contrary; workplace education is booming particularly because of the cost savings associated with online computer-based learning environments. As the Workflow Institute reports, "The overall spending on corporate training in the US will drop from the current $65 billion to around $50-55 billion by 2008. This cost savings will not be at the expense of training workers. New cost-effective methods are being deployed."[14]

RESEARCHING THE VALUE OF INTANGIBLE ASSETS

Academic research on intangibles is rich. Next we take a look at just some of the interesting ways in which intangible value is reflected in stock market prices and accounting ratios.

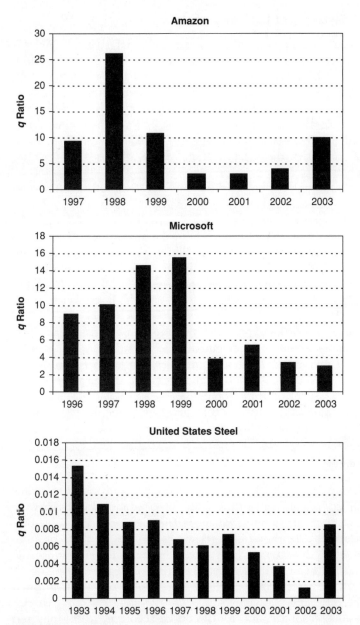

FIGURE 3.4 Tobin's *q* over Time
Sources: Amazon.com SEC Form 10-Ks, 1997 through 2003; United States Steel SEC Form 10-Ks, 1993 through 2003; Microsoft SEC Form 10-K, 1997 through 2003.

Research and Development Expenditures

From a researcher's point of view, the problem with analyzing intangibles is that the requirements for reporting are few and often imprecise. Traditionally R&D expenses have been the only line item intangible expense in public financials that routinely get stated, so the R&D expenditures have been the subject of most academic efforts. Nonetheless, there are some significant results. For example, there is a significant impact on price-to-earnings ratios when expensed R&D costs are adjusted to equivalent capital stock. In R&D-intensive industries, the effect of capitalizing R&D can slash the ratio by more than half.

In addition, although the link between high R&D to future returns has not been strongly established, firms with high R&D-to-market value of equity ratios have shown significant excess annual returns. As might be guessed, performing more R&D for R&D's sake alone does not result in higher returns. The work of University of Illinois researchers Louis Chan, Josef Lakonishok, and Theodore Sougiannis has shown that the amount of return is largely dependent on the sample of firms to begin with: In particular, firms that are "glamour stocks" (those with high market-to-book ratios) do better.[14]

As mentioned, industrial expenditures on R&D, advertising, and personnel are probably around 10 percent of U.S. GDP. The work of John Hand shows that investment in these intangibles also has been profitable. Using the period 1980 through 2000, Hand measured the mean yearly net present value of $1 spent on these intangibles as $0.35, $0.24, and $0.14 respectively. And the profitability of R&D increased from about 16 cents in the 1980s to 50 cents in the 1990s.[16]

Intellectual Capital

Education   During the 1970s, some economists believed that Americans were overqualified. According to this view, college-educated workers were realizing decreasing returns on the value of their education. The wage premium, as measured by the ratio of hourly wages for those with 16 or more years of schooling to those with a high school degree, fell over that decade. Murphy and Welch demonstrate, though, that the college wage premium boomed to over 65 percent in the 1980s. This trend continued, through 1993, with the difference slowing from 1994 through 1997. Figure 3.5 shows these results. What accounts for this effect, according to Murphy and Welch, are the age-old laws of supply and demand. They write:

The story we prefer is one of relatively stable growth in the demand for educated workers over the past three decades with fluctuating

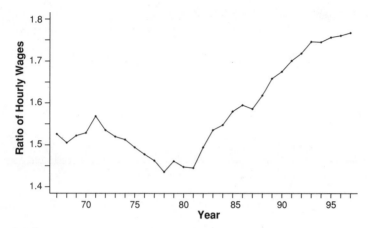

FIGURE 3.5   College Plus/High School Wage Premium, 1967–1997
Sources: Kevin M. Murphy and Finis Welch, "Wage Differentials in the 1990s: Is the Glass Half Full or Half Empty?" in *The Causes and Consequences of Increasing Inequality*, ed. Finis Welch (Chicago: University of Chicago Press, 2001), p. 346.

supply growth generating the observed pattern of changes in wage premiums. Over the 1970s the rapid growth in supply of college workers out-paced demand growth leading to falling relative wages for college graduates while demand growth out-paced supply growth over the 1980s and 1990s.... Changes in technology generate increases in demand for skill. This raises skill premiums and pushes up human capital investment.[17]

Their work also reveals that the inequality in wage premiums is concentrated at the high end of the wage distribution. The wage premium for graduate degrees has been growing throughout the whole period.

Mincer examined the returns to on-the-job training for both employees and employers. Depending on the data sets and other assumptions used, Mincer found employee returns on training to be somewhere between 9 and 31 percent. And, he estimated significant returns for employers, too.[18]

Superstar Scientists   In researching the phenomenal growth in the U.S. biotechnology industry since the 1970s, researchers Lynne Zucker, Michael Darby, and Marilynn Brewer determined that "star" scientists could explain where and when the industry developed. In other words, something beyond location was at work. They write: "Intellectual human capital tended to flourish around great universities, but the existence of outstanding scientists measured in terms of research productivity played a key role over, above, and separate from the presence of those universities and government research funding to them."[19]

Patent Attributes

Accountants and economists struggling with a more direct measure of the value of R&D have examined a number of attributes associated with a firm's patent portfolio. Researchers Zhen Deng, Baruch Lev, and Francis Narin looked at patent counts, citation impact, technology cycle time, and the link to scientific research. Most of the factors they examined were statistically associated with subsequent stock price returns and market-to-book ratios.[20] These results suggest that investors would benefit from knowing more about the details of patent portfolios of firms.

Market Value of Trademarks

Chandrakanth Seethamraju, a professor of accounting at the Olm School of Business at Washington University in Saint Louis, conducted a study to determine if there was valuation-relevant information in estimates of both internally generated and acquired trademarks. He relied on the empirical relationship between trademarks and sales to estimate the value of the internally generated marks, concluding that the values were measurable and significant. Indeed, the mean estimated trademark value in Seethamraju's sample was $580 million, compared to a mean firm book value of $1.7 billion. (The mean market value of the sample was $8.6 billion.) Seethamraju also determined that investors reacted positively to the news that trademarks were being acquired, since these acquisitions could mean larger market share, economies of scale, or increased barriers to competitors entering the market.[21]

The market's reaction to bad news also can be an indicator of a trademark's value. Take, for instance, the decline in Martha Stewart Living Omnimedia stock on the news that Martha Stewart had possibly sold Imclone stock on insider information. This information caused a dilution of anything that was branded Martha Stewart. In one day the stock lost almost 10 percent of its value, nearly $89 million. On the news of her conviction, Martha Stewart's company lost over 22 percent of its value, a nearly $149 million drop. Although these events may be only a subset of the reasons for the total slide in the stock, they most certainly show, to use Tom

Blackett's words, how the company was viewed going forward as unable to keep its promise.

Executive Compensation and Value

The quality of the human capital that manages a firm also has caught the attention of researchers, partly due to the boom in executive compensation, both in absolute size and as a multiple of the "average" worker's wage. Median total realized pay for chief executive officers (CEOs) nearly quadrupled between 1970 and 1996, and the ratio between CEOs and average production workers jumped from 25 times to over 200 times in the same period.[22]

Do the correspondingly better CEOs (with "higher paid" being a stand-in for "better") produce more value for the firm's stockholders? Compensation researchers use a variety of metrics to determine CEO pay. Nearly all of these metrics include accounting measures, and most take into consideration some way to measure EVA, or economic value added. Some include relative performance evaluation vis à vis peer companies. And some take into account, explicitly or implicitly, the stock price of the firm.

But the results are not clear cut. Kevin J. Murphy of USC writes: "It is more difficult to document that the increase in stock-based incentives has led CEOs to work harder, smarter, and more in the interest of shareholders. . . . Many CEOs understand how their actions affect accounting profits, but do not understand how their actions affect shareholder value."[23] Part of the opacity results from efficient capital markets. Investors will adjust the price (down) of a more poorly managed firm to equal the expected risk-adjusted return of a better-managed one.

University of Chicago's Sherwin Rosen addresses why the distribution of CEO pay and firm size is heavily skewed relative to abilities. His research explains seemingly exorbitant CEO pay in terms of the power and influence the CEO has over the rest of the firm. He writes:

> There is a common sense in which chief executive officers of large corporations exercise a great deal of economic power. This power, sometimes labeled responsibility, derives from the influence their decisions exert on the productivity of large numbers of others in the enterprise as a whole. The most capable foot soldier is not very effective if he is fighting the wrong war. Under these circumstances it pays to assign the most talented persons to positions of greatest power and influence. Though other, less talented individuals could manage these organizations, it is inefficient for them to do so. The value of output falls by more than the

opportunity cost of their services in a lower ranking position or in a smaller firm."[24]

Recent research has begun to question the value of having a high-quality, or at least ethical, board of directors and senior managers. With the credibility crisis associated with meltdowns at Arthur Andersen, Enron, WorldCom, and Tyco Industries, and the responsibility imposed on boards by the Sarbanes-Oxley Act of 2002, recent work has attempted to measure the stock price impact of firms that have received below-average or above-average corporate governance ratings. Although the results may not yet be proven empirically, enormous interest in corporate governance tells us that ethics as an intangible asset are now coming under investor scrutiny.

A New Kind of Capital?

In the last decade, many economists and accountants wondered what could explain the explosion in the stock market, given the fact that productivity growth had been minimal and many technology firms were commanding high prices despite having shown little revenue and even less profit. If the market was rational, how could we explain, in the words of Federal Reserve chairman Alan Greenspan, "irrational exuberance"? One creative view was presented by Stanford economist Robert Hall. He proposed the idea that computers and college-educated workers were combining in new ways to create what he termed e-capital.

> *[T]oday's high stock market valuations should be taken seriously as a measure of the resources owned by corporations. I introduce a new kind of capital—e-capital—to characterize these resources.... A firm's e-capital is a body of technical and organizational know-how. Much e-capital involves the use of computers and software, but it is the business methods based on computers, not the computers themselves, that constitute e-capital.*[25]

Hall's concept of e-capital is the result of an accounting information deficit: We are unable to account for the value the stock market places on intangibles just by looking at corporate financial statements. Although e-capital may explain a little less after the Internet bubble burst, it does get us thinking about what intangibles we are missing. Many researchers worry that the hidden effect of the unmeasured intangible assets is greater stock price volatility, which may have the effect of raising the cost of capital for intangible-heavy firms. As this chapter has demonstrated, such firms are not confined to an isolated corner of the Internet. There are intangibles on Main Street, too.

SUMMARY

This chapter discussed the economic characteristics shared by many intangibles. Intangible assets frequently are characterized by high first-copy costs, low or declining marginal costs, and economies of scale. Intangibles often can be consumed by many people at once. There is often imperfect substitution with intangibles, because human capital—especially for superstar athletes, musicians, and scientists—is highly differentiated. Moreover, intangibles can create network effects if they help promote synchronization among users. The text also examined the evidence on the enormous growth in intangible assets, estimated by some at more than $1 trillion per year. It also examined briefly some of the academic research that has attempted to quantify the value associated with investments in intangibles.

CHAPTER 4

Accounting for Intangibles

This chapter summarizes the treatment of intangible assets under the rules promulgated by the Financial Accounting Standards Board (FASB). Intangible assets are discussed at length in various pronouncements, including under current Sections G-40 and I-60 (Accounting Principles Board [APB] 17) as well as in two statements issued on July 20, 2001: Statement No. 141, *Business Combinations*, and Statement No. 142, *Goodwill and Other Intangible Assets*. APB Opinions 16 and 17 largely guided the standards before Financial Accounting Standards (FAS) 141 and 142 were issued.

Financial Accounting Standards (FAS) 141 and 142 heavily impact accounting for intangibles. Previously, when a firm acquired another firm with intangibles, the acquirer would treat all of the target's intangible assets as goodwill, reflected in the excess paid over the net value of the firm's identifiable assets. Goodwill would be capitalized on the balance sheet and then amortized over some (usually long) finite period. Firms were not required to separate from that pool of goodwill any intangibles that could be identified, amortized or not. In general, the only identifiable line-item intangible was research and development (R&D), and that was usually expensed.

For example, in 2001, before the new FASB rules took effect, the main note to the General Motors consolidated financial statements that detailed the firm's intangible assets read:

> *Automotive, Communications Services, and Other Operations had net intangible assets of $13.7 billion and $7.6 billion at December 31, 2001 and December 31, 2000, respectively. At December 31, 2001, net intangible assets consisted primarily of goodwill ($6.8 billion) and pension intangible assets ($6.2 billion). Goodwill is the cost of acquired businesses in excess of the fair value of their identifiable net assets.... Financing and Insurance Operations had net intangible assets of $3.2 billion recorded in other assets, consisting primarily of goodwill, at December 31, 2001 and 2000.*[1]

Other notes throughout the 10-K provided additional information. But to compare apples to apples, by 2002 the same note provided a line each for patents and intellectual property rights, dealer network and subscriber base, customer lists and contracts, trademarks, and covenants not to compete.[2]

If the FASB changed the way intangibles would be recorded in the context of a business combination (i.e., some purchase or merger takes place), undoubtedly it also would change the way intangibles would be recorded for the rest of their lives. In short, this is what FAS 141 and FAS 142 do. Our discussion of the FASB rules covers whether the intangible asset:

- Is identifiable, unidentifiable, or goodwill
- Was acquired or developed internally
- Has an indefinite or finite useful life (and what is the asset's residual value)
- Is subject to amortization or impairment testing
- Should be expensed or capitalized

The gist of the new FASB statements is an increased effort to recognize and value the economic benefits flowing from intangible assets. The statements are driven by the need to determine an intangible asset's *fair value*, which is defined as "the amount at which that asset (or liability) could be bought (or incurred) or sold (or settled) in a current transaction between willing parties, that is, other than in a forced or liquidation sale."[3] As will be demonstrated, this calculation can lead to a paradoxical result: Why would anyone ever pay *more* than fair value?

IDENTIFIABLE AND UNIDENTIFIABLE INTANGIBLE ASSETS

Accounting standards make the distinction whether an intangible asset is identifiable or unidentifiable.

> *An enterprise may acquire intangible assets from others or may develop them itself. Many kinds of intangible assets may be identified and given reasonably descriptive names, for example, patents, franchises, trademarks, and the like. Other types of intangible assets lack specific identifiability. Both identifiable and unidentifiable assets may be developed internally. Identifiable intangible assets may be acquired singly, as a part of a group of assets, or as part of an entire enterprise, but unidentifiable assets cannot be acquired singly. The excess of the cost of an acquired enterprise over the sum of identifiable net assets, usually called goodwill, is the most common unidentifiable intangible asset.[4]*

The key to understanding what is an identifiable intangible is the statement that "unidentifiable assets cannot be acquired singly." We cannot imagine a transaction where management of one firm says to management of another: "We're not interested in acquiring your whole company, but would you sell us just that one thing that we think is valuable, even though we can't put a finger on it?" Therefore, identifiable intangible assets are determined by some criteria of *exchangeability*: Does the asset have legal or contractual status, or can it be sold, transferred, licensed, or rented? Patents, copyrights, trademarks, and trade secrets are certainly identifiable intangible assets because they have legal status. More generally, brands also could be identifiable intangibles; we can easily imagine them being sold or exchanged. FAS 141 goes on to describe criteria for identifying intangible assets as meeting tests of separability or legal-contractual status.

> *The separability criterion is met because the asset is capable of being separated from the acquired entity and sold, transferred, licensed, rented, or otherwise exchanged for something else of value. For example, because an acquired customer list is generally capable of being rented, it meets the separability criterion regardless of whether the acquiring entity intends to rent it.*[5]
>
> *Intangible assets that meet that [contractual legal criterion] shall be recognized apart from goodwill even if the asset is not transferable or separable from the acquired entity or from other rights and obligations.*[6]

With the pronouncement of FAS 141, this exchangeability criteria rose to greater importance. FAS 141 eliminated the pooling-of-interests method of accounting, leaving only the purchase method for all business combinations subsequent to June 30, 2001. The pooling-of-interests method would restate the financials of both companies as if they had always existed as one entity. The purchase method, as its name implies, requires that when an intangible asset is acquired as part of a business combination, that asset gets reported on the financial statements as if it had been bought at its fair value.

But a business need not buy its intangible assets. It also can develop them internally through, for example, R&D efforts, marketing research, or other investments in organizational capital. How are assets valued when there is no purchase? The answer is that the assets are valued as if there would be a purchase—in other words, we calculate the fair value of an arm's-length transaction.

The accounting standards do not specifically prescribe a method for calculating fair value, although they conditionally emphasize that the best available evidence is an active market price. And, although the preferred valuation methodology is one based on a net present value (NPV) calculation, the FASB allows for other calculations as well, as long as the valuation techniques are consistent with the three basic valuation approaches.

Goodwill

Goodwill, the most common unidentifiable intangible asset, comes about as the result of a transaction. It is the "excess of the cost of an acquired enterprise over the sum of identifiable net assets."[7] Goodwill, then, is a residual. But the accounting language does not say it is the *only* unidentifiable intangible asset. It cannot be, because of the (as-yet) unidentifiable assets developed internally. For example, a company may have developed a culture of mentoring that encourages senior executives to impart useful information to younger workers. Suppose that knowledge sharing has helped the company cut design costs. As a result, the company is more profitable than its competitors. If this firm were bought, the mentoring culture would implicitly be lumped into goodwill. In other words, the unidentifiable intangible assets of a firm turn into goodwill if the firm were to be purchased. At this stage, the assets may remain unidentified and continue to be treated as goodwill, or, if possible, they will be identified and separated from goodwill.

Determining Useful Life

Tangible assets wear out, so accounting rules take into account depreciation and amortization, which spread out the value or cost of an asset over some period of time equal to the useful life of the asset. In theory, what is on the balance sheet at any given time is the remaining value of the asset. How the asset was recorded originally usually determines whether it is stated at cost or something else.

Intangibles, too, may have determinate useful lives: "The useful life of an intangible asset to an entity is the period over which the asset is expected to contribute directly or indirectly to the future cash flows of that entity."[8] The FASB goes on to describe various economic considerations that would impact the intangible asset's useful life.

- The expected use of the asset
- Its relationship to the useful lives of other assets
- Legal, regulatory, or contractual provisions that could impact useful life
- The effect of obsolescence, demand, competition, and technological advances
- The level of maintenance expenditures required to obtain the expected future cash flows from the asset

"If no legal, regulatory, contractual, competitive, economic, or other factors limit the useful life of an intangible asset to the reporting entity, the useful life of the asset shall be considered indefinite."[9]

Amortization   Intangibles with finite lives are amortized; goodwill and intangibles with indefinite useful lives are now tested for impairment. FAS 142 introduced this significant change; previously goodwill was amortized, too. Amortization is usually done in a straight line over the remaining useful life, even though the accounting rules do not require linearity. The rules state: "The method of amortization shall reflect the pattern in which the economic benefits of the intangible asset are consumed or otherwise used up." For instance, imagine that a company which licenses a pharmaceutical patent determines that over the remaining five years of the patent's life, new noninfringing substitutes will be introduced in the market, exponentially eroding the sales of the patented good in its remaining years on patent. In this case, it would be appropriate to increase the amount of amortization exponentially each year as the patented product loses share.

The amount actually being amortized "shall be the amount initially assigned to that asset less any residual value."[10] In the case of intangibles, *residual value* usually is assumed to be zero, but again, the rules do not require this, and in fact, scenarios can be imagined where at the end of an asset's useful accounting life, a new entity might purchase the asset for something considerably more than zero. A screenplay, music work, novel, or film's copyright now expires 95 years from publication or 70 years after the death of its creator, but many old stories profitably reemerge in new productions long after their accounting useful life has been used up. For example, *Little Women*, written by Louisa May Alcott, and Rudyard Kipling's *The Jungle Book* both were remade recently into feature films.

Impairment and Indefinitely Lived Assets

If the length of useful life can be reasonably determined, then amortization is the rule. But the life of an intangible asset can be far from clear. A different procedure is followed for those assets that have indefinite lives, to make sure that the recorded value of an intangible is not grossly under- or overstated; intangible assets with indefinite useful lives now are subjected to annual impairment tests. Basically, these tests take an economic look at whether there has been a decline in the asset's fair value.

Accounting rules divide these unamortizable intangible assets into two types: goodwill and everything else. For the everything-else category, which could include a firm's brands or trade secrets, six events or changes in circumstances warrant an impairment loss:

1. A significant decrease in the market price of a long-lived asset (asset group)
2. A significant adverse change in the extent or manner in which a long-lived asset (asset group) is being used or in its physical condition
3. A significant adverse change in legal factors or in the business climate that could affect the value of a long-lived asset (asset group), including an adverse action or assessment by a regulator
4. An accumulation of costs significantly in excess of the amount originally expected for the acquisition or construction of a long-lived asset (asset group)
5. A current-period operating or cash flow loss combined with a history of operating or cash flow losses or a projection or forecast that demonstrates continuing losses associated with the use of a long-lived asset (asset group)
6. A current expectation that, *more likely than not*, a long-lived asset (asset group) will be sold or otherwise disposed of significantly before the end of its previously estimated useful life[11]

For example, when brands are discontinued, the trademark value associated with them becomes impaired. In 2000 General Motors announced it was discontinuing the Oldsmobile line. GM did not separately record the Oldsmobile trademark as an intangible asset, but if it had, it would have required an impairment test (and write-down), just as did the other long-lived assets associated with Oldsmobile, namely the tooling and die machinery that was becoming obsolete.

A more recent and better known example is the disappearance of Paine Webber. In 2002, the Swiss firm UBS wrote down the discontinued Paine Webber brand by nearly $700 million.

Impairment Testing for Goodwill

The impairment testing for goodwill is a little different for three reasons.

1. It is a test of the goodwill of a reporting unit, not some free-standing piece of goodwill.
2. It requires a two-step process.
3. There are more circumstances or events that would reduce the fair value of a reporting unit below its carrying amount than there are for other unamortizable intangible assets, and these require impairment testing *between* annual tests. The FASB states:

The first step of the goodwill impairment test, used to identify potential impairment, compares the fair value of a reporting unit with its carrying amount, including goodwill.... If the fair value of a reporting unit exceeds its carrying amount, goodwill of the reporting unit is considered not impaired, thus the second step of the impairment test is unnecessary. If the carrying amount of a reporting unit exceeds its fair value, the second step of the goodwill impairment test shall be performed to measure the amount of impairment loss, if any.[12]

Reporting Units and Allocating Goodwill   A reporting unit is an operating segment of a company or a component of an operating segment that constitutes a business "for which discrete financial information is available and segment management regularly reviews the operating results of that component."[13] The FASB cares about a reporting unit because the data available at this level enables managers to allocate goodwill with more certainty to the particular economic engines that create it. It states: "Goodwill shall be assigned to the reporting units of the acquiring entity that are expected to benefit from the synergies of the combination."[14]

The method for allocating goodwill to a reporting unit is fairly intuitive; it asks valuers to determine how much of the fair value of the purchase price of the whole entity should be allocated to its various business units. Once the individual assets acquired and liabilities assumed have been identified at the reporting unit level, the difference between their book value and that unit's share of the fair value is the goodwill at the reporting unit. Figure 4.1 gives a representation of the allocation of goodwill to reporting units. It shows the goodwill created from the combination of Firm A and Firm B, with a_1, b_1, and b_2 now the reporting units. Notice, though, that despite being much smaller, b_2 can be allocated a greater amount of goodwill (in both absolute terms and proportionally) because it will benefit most from the combination of Firm A and Firm B. One scenario where this may be true is in a combination of sales forces, where large economies of scale or scope might be realized. Although b_1 is a much larger reporting unit, it may benefit very little from the combination.

Two-Step Test for Goodwill Impairment   Focusing at the reporting unit level, every year we, as valuation analysts, want to ask if the current fair value is greater or less than the carrying amount of that reporting unit including the unit's goodwill. If the fair value is greater, then there is no reason to test the goodwill for impairment. However, if the fair value has declined below the carrying amount including the unit's goodwill, then we undertake the

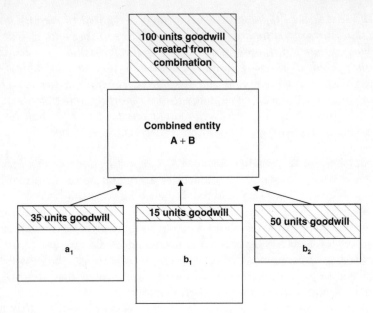

FIGURE 4.1   Reporting Unit Goodwill Allocation.

second step and utilize the impairment tests. By implication, the goodwill may have suffered some decline in value that we have not yet captured. Once adjusted, the carrying amount will no longer overstate the fair value of the reporting unit.

The annual test compares the "implied fair value of the reporting unit goodwill" with the "carrying amount of that goodwill."[15] The implied fair value is determined "as if the reporting unit had been acquired in a business combination."[16] In other words, we check the market value of the reporting unit again. If the goodwill is overstated, then we recognize a goodwill impairment loss.

The FASB also requires that goodwill be tested between annual tests if some significant event has occurred that would *more likely than not* reduce the fair value of the reporting unit below its carrying amount. These events are:

- A significant adverse change in legal factors or in the business climate
- An adverse action or assessment by a regulator
- Unanticipated competition
- A loss of key personnel

- A more-likely-than-not expectation that a reporting unit or a significant portion of a reporting unit will be sold or otherwise disposed of
- The testing for recoverability under Section I08 of a significant asset group within a reporting unit
- Recognition of a goodwill impairment loss in the financial statements of a subsidiary that is a component of a reporting unit[17]

TO EXPENSE OR CAPITALIZE

To recap, before FAS 141 and FAS 142, there were essentially two types of accounting intangibles: identifiable research and development, and unidentifiable goodwill. R&D was expensed as it was incurred. It could include identifiable intangibles, such as patents or trade secrets, but unless revenue was recognized specific to the identifiable assets, the intangibles would not likely be capitalized. Even if a company acquired a firm with identifiable patents, the acquirer would not specifically capitalize the patent assets; instead, they could be part of the goodwill. Goodwill—which came about only through a business combination—would be capitalized on the balance sheet and amortized on the income statement for some finite period.

The accounting world has debated the decision to expense or capitalize intangibles for quite some time. A fair amount of empirical research has been conducted to test the hypothesis that capitalizing some intangible assets would improve financial statement usefulness, which usually is measured as the ability to explain share prices through earnings and book values. Researchers Dennis Chambers, Ross Jennings, and Robert Thompson, for instance, conducted a study that shows that discretionary capitalization and amortization does improve the relevance of financial statements.[18]

But firms often have preferred to expense intangible investments as they occur, writing off the full amount against income immediately, as opposed to capitalizing investments and affecting income only through the periodic depreciation of the asset. One of the ways this is done is through an over-allocation of costs to "in-process" R&D. In the case of an acquisition, GAAP allows the acquirer to write off immediately the expenses the acquired firm has incurred in developing a new product.

Writing just prior to the passage of these new FASB statements, NYU's Baruch Lev, perhaps the world's foremost expert on intangibles accounting, points out that firms have an incentive to expense. He calls this the politics of intangibles. According to Lev: "The major players in the information arena—managers, auditors, financial analysts—are generally comfortable with the current disclosure (rather nondisclosure) environment concerning intangibles. The immediate expensing of internal and acquired R&D, for example, is a recipe for boosting future growth of reported earnings."[19]

Lev notes that even leading software firms Microsoft and Oracle expensed software development costs. He cites evidence that investors do not really consider the one-time write-offs a valuation problem, noting investors' positive reactions to in-process R&D.[20]

What will be interesting to see is how much capitalization of intangibles will result from FAS 141 and FAS 142. These statements have clearly whittled down the amount of goodwill that can be recorded in a business combination or restructuring, and what goodwill is left is now subject to impairment testing. On one hand, firms may expense *more*—they have less freedom to throw identifiable acquired intangibles into goodwill. On the other hand, identifiable intangibles are supposed to be capitalized, too. In any event, FAS 142's resulting impairment testing of goodwill has resulted in some very large write-downs. A notable example is the $54 billion goodwill impairment charge that AOL Time Warner took after AOL acquired Time Warner, followed by an additional $45 billion a year later. Boeing took a $2.7 billion write-down after adopting FAS 142 and then an additional $931 million after restructuring.

Furthermore, when R&D expenses make their way onto the balance sheet, the amount might be included only after a hefty discount. Pfizer, the world's largest pharmaceutical firm (after its acquisition of Pharmacia in 2003), lists "developed technology rights" of over $36 billion as an identifiable asset on its 2003 balance sheet. This means the right "to develop, use, market, sell and/or offer for sale the products, compounds and intellectual property" that Pfizer acquired from Pharmacia. By way of example, one of these products is Bextra, a second-generation COX-2 inhibitor approved for the treatment of arthritis. Pfizer reports that Bextra accounted for almost $700 million in revenues in 2003. But the underlying "developed technology" called valdecoxib is in current R&D projects and also is included in the calculation of balance-sheet value. Pfizer calculates the value using discounted cash flows but is quite clear when it points out that "the projected cash flows of the approved indications [Bextra] are more likely to be achieved than the potential cash flows associated with the R&D projects for the currently unapproved indications. . . . Of the value allocated to developed technology rights, approximately 96% is derived from regulatory-approved uses and indications."[21] If valdecoxib is representative of developed technology rights, then most of its value seems to be included on the balance sheet as Bextra, rather than as a form of capitalized R&D potential.

Some Entertaining Accounting

Record and film companies always have had to address the value of intangible assets because such a large part of their income derives directly from intangible assets. In fact, the accounting conventions followed by enter-tainment firms reveal the dynamic qualities of intangibles. FAS 50, *Financial Reporting in the Record and Music Industry*, states:

> *The portion of the cost of a record master borne by the record company shall be reported as an asset if the past performance and current popularity of the artist provides a sound basis for estimating that the cost will be recovered from future sales. Otherwise, that cost shall be charged to expense. The amount recognized as an asset shall be amortized over the estimated life of the recorded performance using a method that reasonably relates the amount to the net revenue expected to be realized.*[22]

Motion picture studios also follow accounting rules that implicitly recognize different tranches of risk associated with the revenues and costs of their business. These rules guide when revenues can be recognized from the production of films for theatrical release or television, as well as rules for determining capitalizing or expensing production costs. Some excerpts from SFAS 53, *Financial Reporting by Producers and Distributors of Motion Picture Films*, make clear this logic:

> *Production costs ordinarily are accumulated by individual films in four chronological steps: (a) acquisition of the story rights; (b) preproduction, which includes script development, costume design, and set design and construction; (c) principal photography, which includes shooting the film; and (d) postproduction which includes sound synchronization, and editing, culminating in a completed master negative. . . .*
>
> *Either a classified or unclassified balance sheet may be presented. If a classified balance sheet is presented, film costs shall be segregated on the balance sheet between current and noncurrent assets. The following film costs shall be classified as current assets: unamortized costs of film inventory released and allocated to the primary market, completed films not released (reduced by the portion allocated to secondary markets), and television films in production that are under contract of sale. All other capitalized film costs shall be classified as noncurrent assets.*
>
> *The components of film inventories (including films released, completed but not released, and in process and story rights and scenarios) shall be disclosed.*[23]

Software Accounting

Software, too, is an intangible with its own set of accounting rules. Generally, computer software that is developed for research and development purposes is treated as an R&D expense. Software that is developed internally for non–R&D purposes, though, would not be so treated. An example of this kind of development would be software that was created to improve the efficiency of a firm's accounting or marketing departments. That software development cost would be expensed under those departments.

But firms that plan on selling software have different rules. Those firms are largely guided by Financial Accounting Statement 86 (FAS–86), which states that until a point of technical feasibility is reached, the firm should expense the costs of developing the software. Then, after technical feasibility has been established, all costs are capitalized until the product is ready for the market, at which time the costs are amortized. (Again, amortization requires some economic estimate of remaining useful life.) So what is technical feasibility? The short answer is a working model, one that has made it through the basics of coding, testing, and design stages.

Where software really gets interesting is in accounting for the inventory. What does it mean to have a large inventory of software available for sale, given what we know about scalability—the low cost of just "printing up some more inventory"? It may (and probably does) mean that we would expect to see relatively low inventory values for software firms. Master copies and packaging do not account for the lion's share of the value of a software product. After all, those are the tangible parts.

A Brief Note on the International Financial Reporting Standards

Outside of the United States, a different set of accounting rules are used. The International Accounting Standards (IAS), which are now called the International Financial Reporting Standards (IFRS), represent the standards followed by the European Union, Australia, and many emerging economies. There are some differences with the latest GAAP standards, so comparing the same company's financial statements using GAAP or IFRS would not give the same results. In general, GAAP standards recognize economic rights for a firm to classify intangibles, whereas IFRS more strictly depends on legal criteria. Although goodwill is no longer amortized under GAAP, it is still amortized under IFRS (usually to a maximum of 20 years). Probably the most significant difference is in the expensing of R&D: Under GAAP, in-process R&D is immediately expensed, while under IFRS, R&D is capitalized and amortized. Standard-setting boards of the two agencies recognize the need to move the standards closer together, but at this time the differences remain.

GOODWILL PARADOX: WHY PAY MORE THAN FAIR VALUE?

As we have seen, goodwill is nothing more than the "extra" someone pays for a company above the fair value of the identifiable assets. Now, with FAS 141 and FAS 142, the inclusion of identifiable intangibles makes goodwill smaller. The question is: Why would there ever be any "extra"? Why would anyone ever pay more than the fair value of something? Don't the recent FASB changes assure us that the fair value of goodwill does not exceed its carrying value?

There could be three reasons to pay more than "fair value":

1. Misidentification
2. Mismeasurement
3. Uncertainty.

There could be misidentification, a disagreement about what counts as an identifiable intangible asset. The exchangeability criteria require judgment. For example, the buyers may consider some customer acquisition costs as an investment rather than an expense—even if other analysts evaluating the assets under GAAP accounting would not.

There also could be mismeasurement. We might agree with the identification of some firm's intangibles, but we might think that discounted cash flow approach to measuring its fair value is not as good as, say, the price of other recently sold pieces of similar intangibles. Or we might think that comparable intangibles cannot be reliably found in the current market. How valuable, for instance, is a patent on three-dimensional imaging technology? The previous sales of such assets may give us only a rough idea of the patent's value, or even when in that patent's life it may prove valuable to commercialize.

Another reason for paying more than fair value is that the buyers may know that the target has developed internally (as-yet) unidentifiable intangible assets. They recognize the target's ability to achieve some unexplained economic benefit, and they are willing to pay for the unidentifiable assets. When they purchase this firm, they will be converting those unidentifiables into goodwill. In other words, a certain amount of uncertainty is present when buyers are on the outside looking in. Sometimes a willing buyer will pay for it.

SUMMARY

This chapter examined the treatment of intangible assets under GAAP accounting. In particular, it looked at how two relatively recent changes promulgated by the Financial Accounting Standards Board, FAS 141 and FAS 142, have impacted accounting for intangibles. In general, the rules have made goodwill less of a catchall. Intangibles that can be identified need to be capitalized on their own. Intangibles also are divided into those with determinant lives and those that, in theory, can provide benefits indefinitely. The latter type now is required to be tested annually for impairment.

The current accounting regulations do a better job at allowing us to count various items as intangible assets. They also allow us to reevaluate those intangibles over time by requiring them to be stated at fair value. But it still leaves goodwill as a place-holder for economic benefits that we are willing to pay for but cannot quite pinpoint. Is there more we could do to understand value? The next chapter on the portfolio of intangible economic benefits develops this concept in more detail.

CHAPTER **5**

Portfolio of Intangible Economic Benefits (PIE-B)

*Too often one hears that it is impossible to value intangibles
and that, therefore, no change should be made in current
corporate disclosures. This argument reflects the confusion
of the measurement and disclosure issues. The difficulties in
valuing intangibles—a measurement issue—should not preclude
the disclosure in footnotes to financial reports or by other
means of factual, important information, such as on investment
technology, employee training, customer acquisition costs, and
Internet activities.*
        —Baruch Lev, *Intangibles: Management, Measurement,
        and Reporting*

The preface to this book stated that the patent portfolio of a pharmaceutical firm and a college education are both intangible assets. At that early
stage we gave no detailed explanation of how this could be, only that the
chief executive officer (CEO) interested in selling his firm's patents and the
parents of the college-bound youngster both were facing an economic decision. Both were interested in costs and benefits; both wondered which path
would lead to a higher value.

Readers also might recall that the assets were definitely intangible.
Touching them was not important (or even possible); rather, the property
rights associated with owning the assets created the value. Property rights
have value (when they have value at all) if owning them will result in some
above-average return, some greater pleasure, some extra utility. Herein lies
the basis for constructing a firm's portfolio of intangible economic benefits,
or PIE-B for short.

PROTO-ASSETS

Anything that we hypothesize produces an above-average return is potentially as an asset. We say potentially because, after analysis, it may turn out that some things yield no clearly discernable benefits. Between not qualifying and meeting accounting standards lie *proto-assets*. Figure 5.1 depicts the relationship for a hypothetical firm Test Company. Remember the gray area from the figure in Chapter 2? The gray area represents Test Company's proto-assets.

We adopt the term "proto-assets" because it avoids the specific accounting definition—in other words, we are not so sure about these that we know how to treat them according to generally accepted accounting principles (GAAP); and it avoids *too* imprecise language—in other words, we do not mean to include everything, only items that are positive along a couple of dimensions. These dimensions are the focus of this chapter.

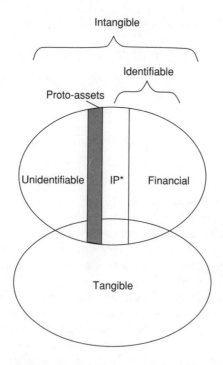

*Intellectual Property

FIGURE 5.1   Test Company's Assets.

INTRODUCING THE PIE-B

The PIE-B serves as a supplemental balance sheet, a place where we can record things[1] that add value. If the firm we are examining is put up for sale, the PIE-B should help us parse out the value of any goodwill above fair value that could be attributed to particular proto-assets, such as customer lists or internally generated research and development. The PIE-B is a place both for disclosure and, when possible, actual valuation. To construct a firm's PIE-B, we have to answer two questions about each thing under consideration:

1. Who owns it, and to what extent?
2. Does it generate economic benefits?

Figure 5.2 depicts the framework for analysis along these two dimensions.

Ownership

For the easily identifiable intangibles, answering the first question is a relatively straightforward task. Take Test Company's copyrights. The firm certainly owns them. There is no mystery here about the copyrights' legal status—not unless, of course, that status is challenged in a lawsuit.

But let us return to the college education example for a little more creative analysis. It is four years later. Our student chose to attend the private university and has now graduated. She certainly has had the benefit of the college education, but does she own it if her parents paid for her schooling? What if the military paid for her schooling? In this case, tuition expenditure does not provide direct ownership of the asset, the expenditure of labor in

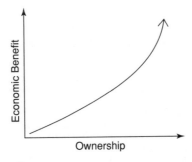

FIGURE 5.2 Two Dimensions of PIE-B.

postsecondary education does: attending classes, doing homework, writing papers, taking tests, and so on. Someone else might have financed the education, but there is no question that she personally claims the degree because she supplied the labor input necessary to meet the university's degree criteria. In the case of the military, the investment means a right to use the educated student asset for some period of time.

Now consider a more complex example of the CEO of the pharmaceutical firm. Does the firm own the CEO, his brainpower, his degrees? Not unless the CEO is an indentured servant (and this does not mean "golden handcuffs"). Indeed, if the CEO were fired, the degrees would go with him. Yet the firm does have use of the CEO's brainpower and education as long as it employs him. To be able to uniquely appropriate economic benefits from the CEO, the firm probably will bind the CEO with noncompete agreements and will motivate him to stay by the structure of his compensation package, just like the college student's deal with the military. The noncompete agreements are the proto-assets because they increase the firm's ownership of the CEO's service.

These situations point out that the degree of ownership is a key factor in answering the first question. *Portability* is an important characteristic. Literally, an analyst can ask whether a firm's assets have feet, or whether the assets walk out the door every day at 5 p.m. (This distinction was discussed in Chapter 2, under the characteristics of intellectual capital and organizational capital.) The extent of ownership varies with the extent or ease of portability. On one extreme, there is no doubt about whether a firm owns a particular proto-asset. On the other extreme, the firm may have little confidence in its ability to count something as its own. Figure 5.3 depicts this relationship.

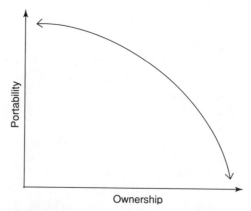

FIGURE 5.3   Ownership versus Portability.

The scale on which portability is measured is not simply a legal one. It is also economic. There may be no legal contract requiring the CEO to stay at the hypothetical pharmaceutical firm; he may be free to leave whenever he wishes to join the competition. One would want to know more about the likelihood of that occurring. For instance, the firm may provide some benefit to the CEO, such as an incomparable location, or the fact that relatives also work at the company, which makes his leaving unlikely. (Of course, depending on your relatives, that might make leaving more likely!) Those tying factors in turn could be considered proto-assets. They might not be as readily apparent as a noncompete agreement, but they could be even more important. In any case, they slide the CEO up the firm's scale of ownership.

Information about the extent of ownership is important in valuation. One method for measuring something in the PIE-B that is less than fully owned would be to assign it a probability of "walking." For example, the firm might assign a probability of losing the CEO as only 25 percent. Put another way, the firm might be able to count 75 percent of the value of the CEO along the dimension of ownership. A more sophisticated approach would consider the probability of "walking" under different scenarios, each with its own probability. But what is the value along the second dimension?

Economic Benefit

Economic benefit is the second criteria in the PIE-B analysis. For simplicity's sake, assume for the moment that identification is not an issue, that the proto-asset is not portable. Consider the college graduate's choice of school. Leaving inflation, discounting, and other costs out of the equation, her total tuition expenditure was $120,000. If she had chosen the public college, tuition would have totaled $28,000, for a difference of $92,000. Is the private school worth the difference?

College Student's Benefits   One approach might be to consider the difference in her expected income streams, depending on which school she attended. Suppose that graduates of the private university earn 10 percent more than their public college counterparts. If that difference of 10 percent totaled up over a lifetime is more than the difference in tuition, we might conclude that the expense was justified, that the investment in the private school education generated value in the form of excess economic benefits.

Without getting into too many details of the calculation here (inflation, the discount rate, the extrapolation to a time series), actual data seems to support the conclusion. In 1997 the average income for *private university* bachelor's degree recipients four years after graduating was $38,306, while the same income for *public college* bachelor's degree recipients four years after graduating was $31,967.[2] So, the difference between the private university and the public college is about 15 percent, or $6,000. If we assume for simplification that the premium on the four-year earnings figure continues unchanged, it would take working for about 21 years to break even on the education investment.[3]

While there are many good public colleges and many poor private universities, on average this result is what we might expect. A top university (here also a private one) should have a positive net present value (NPV) associated with attending in order to attract top students. Of course, top students can attend weaker schools, but usually weak students cannot attend top schools. Furthermore, our example counts only the cost of tuition as the investment. Part of the higher return associated with good schools comes from the extra efforts. The example also ignores many other important benefits that could come with attending either school. Chicago's Gary Becker reminds us that there are nonmonetary benefits to education: "Many studies show that education promotes health, reduces smoking, raises the propensity to vote, improves birth control knowledge, and stimulates the appreciation of classical music, literature, and even tennis."[4]

CEO's Benefit Now let us consider the pharmaceutical firm's CEO. Does the CEO proto-asset generate economic benefits? At least on the surface this analysis is straightforward. We want to compare our CEO to CEOs at other firms. Does ours generate more income for the firm? Does he save the firm more money? Does the added income or cost savings offset the salary he is paid? We could use either the income approach from Chapter 6 or the market approach from Chapter 7.

Assume (unrealistically!) for now that the results are crystal clear: Test Company makes $10 million per year in profit, and our CEO is personally responsible for generating 10 percent ($1 million) per year more in profit than other CEOs. No matter where he goes, he is always able to generate that excess profit above the salary he is paid. We might say, then, that the noncompete agreements—the proto-assets we wish to tally in the PIE-B—are worth that $1 million per year, discounted to today. But we must count only 75 percent of that discounted $1 million because of the 25 percent chance assigned to walking—to the firm not really being able to lay claim to the CEO as an asset. Thus, the PIE-B value of the CEO is a discounted $750,000.

Even with this gross simplification, it is still not clear what it is about this particular man that is valuable. It might be his academic background, his network of well-connected business associates, his charisma or ability to motivate workers, or it might be the whole package, something we could call the CEO's brand. As we learned in Chapter 3, understanding how a CEO contributes is important. Writing in response to a fund manager's proposal that CEO compensation be restricted to no more than 100 times that of the average employee, Cendant (one of the Catholic Fund's targets) replied to the Securities and Exchange Commission: "How will the company distinguish between those achievements stemming from the C.E.O.'s contribution versus those that are a result of favorable economic conditions or other factors?"[5] Exactly.

In the real world, it is a lot harder to attribute results with certainty. So, we should record the CEO as a proto-asset. We know he adds something— positive along the economic benefits dimension; and we know he is relatively certain to stay put—positive along the ownership dimension.

PERSPECTIVES ON THE PIE-B

This text is not the first to conceptualize intangible assets that are off–balance sheet, nor is it a unique idea to think about quantifying them. Accountants, financial writers, brand valuation experts, and economists consider concepts quite similar to the PIE-B . Some of these concepts focus on intangible assets, while others are frameworks whose purpose is to measure economic benefit more broadly and, in so doing, incorporate a firm's intangibles, too. These collective efforts often are considered to comprise a firm's *economic balance sheet*. Let us explore some of these methods. For example, what would a brand valuation expert do with the CEO?

A Brand Valuation Model

Brands are properly recognized as much more than a name or a legal conceptualization, such as the trademark. Brand consultants use specific methods for measuring brand value off the balance sheet. Interbrand, Omnicom's branding subsidiary, utilizes a four-stage methodology that translates into part of our PIE-B framework. It includes:

1. A segment analysis, which groups the brand according to how it is manifested to the customer (in our language, finding the proto-asset characteristics).
2. A financial analysis, which identifies business earnings (PIE-B's economic benefit dimension).
3. An analysis to determine what proportion of those business earnings are attributable to the brand (PIE-B's ownership dimension).
4. A brand strength analysis, which assesses the security of the brand franchise; this analysis is expressed as a brand strength score, which provides a discount rate to apply to brand earnings (also part of the PIE-B ownership calculation).[6]

Brand strength, in turn, is measured along seven attributes:

1. Market
2. Stability
3. Leadership
4. Trend
5. Support
6. Geography
7. Protection

A brand valuation of the CEO would combine these analyses to determine the incremental benefit the CEO's brand provides and then would discount it relative to a CEO of average ability.

The Interbrand model does not provide any easy answers—it is still going to be most difficult to assign a proportion of value to the CEO. (A real valuation requires more than a seat-of-the-pants estimate of 10 percent of excess profit.) Nonetheless, the model adds some interesting insight, especially in the calculation of the discount rate and how that can change over time as a brand ages. A young, untested brand, say Coca-Cola of 100 years ago, has a far higher risk profile than Coca-Cola of today. And while Marlboro today may not be any less risky than it was 100 years ago, it certainly does not hold the promise of its former self.

Danish Experience

Some 17 Danish firms that participated in the creation of the Danish Agency for Trade and Industry's *Guideline for Intellectual Capital Statements*[7] put in place something very much like the PIE-B. These statements reveal a profound understanding that there is more to the value of firms than can be expressed on balance sheets. According to appendix 3 of the guidelines, "The objective of the intellectual capital statement is to state the company's resource basis and explain the activities the management puts into action to develop it."

Most relevant to mention here are the Danish firms' collection of indicators. These are metrics used to count intangibles. Some worth mentioning are:

- Proportion of staff with a university degree
- Training investment per employee
- Staff turnover
- Social events including theme days (show what the company does to increase employees' social network)

- Cooperation agreements with universities and business schools
- Number of currently approved patents
- Shared knowledge documents on the Internet
- Product innovation rate

Take, for example, the number and character of cooperation agreements that a business has with universities. These may be formal knowledge-sharing agreements, or they might be right-of-first-refusal licensing arrangements. They also might be informal but nonetheless important network relationships between university researchers and company executives. We should include them in the PIE-B. Such agreements would rate highly on the ownership scale. Then we would need to measure their value along the benefits side, which would involve one of the valuation approaches in the next chapters.

To give readers a preview, we might compare income attributable to projects that came about from the university connection to those the firm generated on its own. Or we might compare this firm's relationships to those of its competitors' and devise a way to quantify the economic impact they have. Better lead flow, higher royalties, fewer vulnerable patents, reduced research and development expenditures, and lower recruiting costs are just some of the ways that good relationships with a university might translate into measurable benefits over a firm without those connections. It is not a coincidence that many innovative smaller firms locate in research parks at or near major academic institutions. Areas such as Boston's 128 Corridor, Chapel Hill's Research Triangle, and Silicon Valley or Sand Hill sprout intermediary technology and venture capital firms that often turn university research into marketplace products.

Accounting Perspective

Once we have determined that there is a nonzero value along both the ownership and economic benefit metrics, the intangible factor becomes a proto-asset. But the relationship between various intangibles need not follow a pattern. Although it is true that some proto-assets are more weakly owned than others, and some proto-assets are farther along in terms of generating hard, cold economic benefits, it is not true that younger or weaker intangibles evolve into more mature ones or that they will look familiar when they are mature. Often proto-assets cannot be patented, copyrighted, or trademarked. Workplace camaraderie, for example, is more ethereal than a secret. But it does have value.

As we touched on in Chapter 4, in accounting, this idea plays out in the decision whether to expense or capitalize what we would call a proto-asset. As we move along the scale of increasing ownership and increasing benefit, accounting conventions generally would have us move the asset onto the balance sheet.

This accounting convention is really no different from our two-dimensional model of portability and economic benefit, with the distinction that the accounting rules are not continuous. Assets are classified by the particular characteristics that govern whether expensing them as costs or capitalizing them as assets is appropriate. At first blush, the classification may seem crude. But there are good reasons for prohibiting too much accounting creativity—at least in the financial statements of publicly traded firms. Outside investors want to know that the method used at different firms for valuing assets is the same, even if this consistency may make balance sheet values less meaningful. It is difficult enough to be certain that firms capitalize tangible assets similarly. If we cannot be certain that each firm has the same way of assigning value to a proto-asset, then we will only cloud comparisons about the relative value of each firm. Indeed, commentators are undecided on the net effects of the Financial Accounting Statements (FAS) 141 and 142. On one hand, the rules provide much-needed detail about intangibles; on the other hand, there is wiggle room for firms to make disclosures about their intangibles when they see fit—not necessarily as soon as investors might want.

Disclosure Benefits

NYU's Lev argues that disclosing as much as possible about a firm's intangible assets is not only in the interest of the investor, it is also in the interest of the firm. Lev underscores the theory of inevitable disclosure: If one believes that most information eventually is revealed in efficient capital markets, those who reveal more information sooner are interpreted as better managers and, hence, are rewarded by the market with higher valuations, presumably because investors believe such companies are less risky. Lev's proposal to assist in disclosure is called the Value Chain Scoreboard. It is a framework for classifying intangibles in three stages of development: discovery and learning, implementation, and commercialization. For most firms, each stage would represent increasing certainty along the PIE-B's economic benefit dimension. For example, under discovery and learning, Lev counts "internal renewal" (like R&D and workforce training); under implementation, he places "intellectual property" (i.e., patents and trademarks); and under commercialization lies "customers" (e.g., brand values) and "performance" (i.e., revenues, earnings, market share, and royalties).[8]

SUMMARY

The most important feature of the PIE-B is that it represents an effort to analyze intangibles that is not required or even permitted by the accounting rules. The Danish government's initiative listed many benefits from the process to create intellectual capital statements. It cites the organization's creating of a culture of knowledge sharing, positive external signaling to customers and investors, as well as creating a common identity—all themes that sound remarkably similar to what branding experts refer to as the benefits of brand strategy and what Lev captures in the Value Chain Scoreboard.

Most of our discussion has been about fitting human capital into the PIE-B. In general, it is more difficult to identify and measure human capital than intangibles such as patents, copyrights, or trademarks. But the same themes apply to more identifiable assets—those that are probably just farther up the ownership scale.

Last, it should not surprise readers that few firms would publish their PIE-B. It is hardly always to a firm's advantage to reveal everything it considers to be a proto-asset. Firms may treat their proto-assets much like trade secrets. At times it makes sense to keep some things from one's competitors. This is true even if a firm is public—firms always weigh a disclosure's inevitability against the value of keeping a secret. In other words, it is not really the firm's job to reveal as much as it can, but it is our job, as investors, analysts, and scholars, to *learn* as much as we can.

CHAPTER **6**

Income Approach
and Intangibles

So far we have explored the terminology of intangible assets, some economic characteristics, some evidence of their value, the most important accounting rules for dealing with intangibles, and even a conceptual framework to prepare intangible assets for measurement. Now it is time to explore the first of three valuation techniques. Again, before embarking on our exploration of the different approaches, we should endeavor to remember that the best valuation attempts to reconcile all approaches.

This chapter presents the basic steps of calculating present value. Then it extends the example into a hypothetical intangible that we are going to value with the income approach. This analysis moves from the tangible to the intangible assets reflected in Test Company's proverbial soda pop machine. At the end, we arrive at a value of the intangible proto-asset that can be tallied in Test Company's portfolio of intangible economic benefits, or PIE-B. It will require valuing three different streams of income:

1. The income from soda pop sales to employees
2. The inefficiency (lost income) currently caused by the machine's presence
3. Income that could result from the machine's intangible asset

After we work through this theoretical example, this chapter goes on to discuss some particular issues when applying the income approach to intangibles. We also discuss how the entertainment industry provides some guidance and how options pricing can be a helpful alternative. At the end of the chapter is an appendix that goes into more detail about calculating the discount rate. But first let us tackle some basics.

73

STEPS TO THE INCOME APPROACH

The income approach to valuing an intangible asset is a straightforward application of the discounted cash flow (DCF) methodology. At its core, the aim is to figure out how much something is worth today based on how much it will return in the future. The return is the income or cash flows. Why the income approach "works," is rooted in some very basic financial principles:

- All else equal, investors will pay more for investments that generate more cash flow.
- All else equal, investors will pay more for investments that generate their cash flows sooner (Time Value of Money).
- All else equal, investors will pay more for investments whose cash flows are less risky.

With these as our guide as to what matters to investors (or in this case the CEO of Test Company), our methodology will employ three steps. To use it we must:

1. Identify the asset from which we are trying to derive economic benefit.
2. Estimate the expected cash flows from that asset over time.
3. Assign an appropriate measure of risk to our prediction.

Notice that the method does not specify whether an asset is intangible or not. This is important. The basic approach is no different for intangibles than it is for tangible assets. What *is* different is the attention required to apply an income approach to intangibles.

Identification, the first step, can be particularly difficult with intangibles. It is pretty easy to spot the widget-molding device in the room; it is not so clear where the widget operator's know-how is.

In the second step we attempt to isolate the value that can be attributed to the asset (or proto-asset) under review. Identifying and measuring are two sides of the same coin. In other words, when we have assigned some income to, say, the widget operator's know-how, we are making a statement about our ability to both identify and quantify the know-how.

In the second step we also have to predict how much the asset will return in each future period. Shortcut assumptions may be wholly inadequate. There is no law that the returns remain constant, increase at some linear rate, or decrease in some predictable way. Further, we have to decide when the asset's useful life is up. Or can it produce value indefinitely? The often indeterminant life of an intangible asset is another distinction to make from tangibles.

In the third step we have to take stock of our prediction. Are the cash flows we have settled on a sure bet, or does the income stream look like wild speculation? How much of that risk is specific to the asset, the company, or the market? We also have to recognize the time value of money. Here is where the discount rate is applied to the cash flows.

PRESENT VALUE FORMULA

The present value of a cash flow for one period out into the future is written as:

$$PV = \frac{C_1}{1 + r_1}$$

where PV = present value
C_1 is the cash flow in period 1
r_1 is the discount rate in period 1

(Don't worry—we'll explain the discount rate below.) For three periods, the present value would look something like:

$$PV = \frac{C_1}{1 + r_1} + \frac{C_2}{1 + r_2} + \frac{C_3}{1 + r_3}$$

For t periods, the equation is:

$$PV = \sum \frac{C_t}{1 + r_t}$$

If the cash flows are presumed to occur in the same amount at the same discount rate every year, then we value them as a perpetuity. The formula is:

$$PV = \frac{C_i}{r_i}$$

Of course, these formulas show only the future cash flows from some existing asset. Frequently, the valuation is made to decide whether to acquire the asset. When we include the cost to acquire the asset, we are calculating the *net present value* (NPV). The formula looks like this:

$$NPV = C_0 + \sum \frac{C_t}{(1 + r_t)^t}$$

Cash Flows from the Tangible Asset

Let us first work with the soda pop machine as a tangible asset to explain where C and r come from. Some people in the firm have suggested that Test Company should do away with the machine. Often large crowds gather around it a couple of times a day talking about sports scores, celebrities, or local news. Some have argued that the machine has become a distraction, pulling people away from their jobs and creating inefficiencies.

Test Company's chief executive officer (CEO) first decides to value the cash flows from the sale of soda pop. The company does not pay anything for the machine. It is supplied for free by the soda distributor, who makes money on a percentage of the sales of soda. The CEO wants to measure the future revenues associated with the machine. For every can of soda sold, Test Company makes 5 cents in profit. There are no supply constraints; Test Company can get as much soda from the distributor as it needs. Test Company has not changed much in size over the last 15 years, and its 100 employees are extremely predictable as far as thirst-quenching goes. In fact, if Test Company's CEO predicted each of his 100 employees drank on average two sodas a day for the next three years, he would be very accurate. Although it is a simplification to analyze the cash flows annually, and another simplification to consider only three years, it will suffice for demonstration purposes. The soda machine cash flows would look something like this:

$$(100 \text{ employees}) \times (2 \text{ sodas a day}) \times (250 \text{ work days per year}) \times (3 \text{ years}) \times \$0.05 = \$7,500$$

Of course, the company does not receive all the soda revenue in one lump sum now. The distributor cuts one check at the end of each year. The CEO is interested in accounting for the time and risk associated with the cash flows. To do this he needs to calculate the *discount rate*. But where does the discount rate come from?

The Discount Rate

Analysts spend an enormous amount of effort to determine what is the correct discount rate to use when calculating the present value of cash flows. Indeed, financial theorists have developed some famous and useful concepts in this area: the capital assets pricing model (CAPM), arbitrage pricing theory (APT), the Fama-French Three Factor Model, and others. A detailed explanation of which model to use in calculating the discount rate is beyond the scope of this text, although we will address the basics in the appendix to this chapter.

Regardless of which model we choose, however, no model can fix incorrectly identified cash flows, a mistake that happens when analysts confuse the kind of risk that can be discounted. Project-specific risk (also called *diversifiable risk*) cannot be addressed by arbitrarily goosing up the discount rate. Market risk (also called *systematic risk*) is what the discount rate incorporates.

Recognizing what is risky about a specific project is especially important for taking into account the sometimes wildly fluctuating cash flows of intangible assets. Think of the cash flows of businesses that invest in untried filmmakers, recording artists, fashion designers, or software engineers! Cash flows in the income approach often are described as *unbiased*; they need to factor in bad outcomes as well as good ones. The correct cash flows include the possibility that the movie flops, that the record produces no hits, that the fashion trend never catches on, and that the software is buggy. Therefore, the mantra of this text is: *First get the cash flows right.*[1] Then worry about the discount rate.

In its simplest form, the discount rate we calculate is Test Company's *opportunity cost of capital.* Suppose that Test Company has the opportunity to make an investment in a new candy bar machine. If investing in the candy bar machine is more profitable, then the soda machine "investment" looks relatively unattractive—hence we apply a discount to soda sales.

ESTIMATING THE DISCOUNTED CASH FLOWS

To bring all the pieces together, we will use the capital assets pricing model (CAPM). Academics and analysts argue about whether the CAPM is the best method, but it is widely used and provides a good starting point for thinking about how to integrate the types of risk. The CAPM formula can be written as:

The expected risk premium on an asset = the asset beta × the expected risk premium on the market

Or, with notation:

$$r_i - r_f = \beta_i \times (r_m - r_f)$$

where
r_f = the risk-free rate
B_i = beta of the asset
r_m = expected return on the market
$r_m - r_f$ = expected premium on the market

We can rearrange the formula so that r_i will be our discount rate:

$$r_i = r_f + \beta_i \times (r_m - r_f)$$

Calculating the Soda Machine Income

We will assume that the risk-free rate is 2 percent ($r_f = 2$). The expected market return is 8 percent ($r_m = 8$), so the expected risk premium on the market is $8 - 2$, or 6. We will assume the asset beta is 1. Beta measures how much the project (or asset) return varies with the market return. For example, a beta of 2 is twice as volatile; a beta of 0.5 is half as volatile. (Beta is covered in more detail in the appendix to this chapter.) The discount rate can be calculated as:

$$r_i = 2 + [1 \times (8 - 2)] = 8$$

The DCF for the soda cash flows for three years looks like this:

$$\frac{\$2,500}{(1 + 8\%)} + \frac{\$2,500}{(1 + 8\%)^2} + \frac{\$2,500}{(1 + 8\%)^3} = \$2,314 + \$2,143 + \$1,985$$
$$= \$6,443$$

It is easy to see the effect of the discount rate. Instead of $7,500 over three years, it turns out that Test Company's machine really is generating more than $1,000 less. The bigger the discount rate and the longer the time period, obviously the bigger an effect there will be on the cash flows. After 20 years, this discount rate would reduce the cash flows by half—instead of $50,000, the present value would be only $24,545. As a perpetuity, the cash flows are equal to only $31,250.

Calculating the Lost Wages

Having determined the income directly attributable to soda sales, the next step Test Company's CEO takes is to estimate the cost in terms of the inefficiency of having the machine in the company break room. He figures that each employee probably spends a total of 15 minutes each day standing around the machine. About half of the employees properly record this time "off the clock." The firm is paying the other employees for their break time. Although neither group is making widgets while they are on break, the cost comes from those who cheat—they are being paid for their time, and they also are not producing widgets. If the average wage rate at Test Company is $10 per hour, then the cost of the inefficiency looks something like this:

Lost productivity of off-the-clock employees = 50 employees × ¼ hour
= 12.5 hours per day

Lost wages = 12.5 hours per day × $10 per hour = $125 per day

$125 per day × 250 days per year = $31,250 per year

Using the DCF formula, the CEO calculates that over three years this costs the firm:

$$\frac{\$31,250}{1.08} + \frac{\$31,250}{(1.08)^2} + \frac{\$31,250}{(1.08)^3} = \$80,534$$

To calculate the discount rate for the lost wages, the CEO uses the opportunity cost of capital associated with Test Company's widget manufacturing line. This may not be the same as the opportunity cost of the soda machine revenue. (Because our example is completely hypothetical, though, we will assume that those opportunity costs are the same.)

At first, it seems that removing the soda machine will eliminate more than $74,000 in inefficiencies. (This is simply $80,534 less $6,443.) For those interested, if the cash flows are calculated in perpetuity, it would look even better: $391,000 less $31,000. But the CEO knows there is more to his employees' thirst. If the firm got rid of the machine, the CEO is pretty certain that at least half of the employees would still take a break to buy a drink at the nearby convenience store down the block from Test Company's plant. He figures that at least half the employees would still demand a soda per day. This means 25 employees will take an on-the-clock trip to the local convenience store. If each trip is still 15 minutes, Test Company would save only half of the lost wages, so that in the world but for the soda machine, the net effect of eliminating it would be:

$$\frac{\$80,534}{2} - \$6,443 = \$33,824$$

The CEO realizes that his calculations are pretty rough, but the result seems compelling: Test Company would save almost $34,000 from eliminating the soda machine. Is there something he is missing?

SODA MACHINE AS PROTO-ASSET?

There is one more important feature of the soda pop machine. The CEO has noticed that the full range of Test Company's employees gather around the machine during their breaks. Why, he himself regularly drinks soda in the break area talking with management, widget makers, and shipping personnel. Recently he overheard a conversation between the packaging manager and the shipping clerk in which they were discussing an easier way to produce the boxes that hold widgets. In fact, for every discussion about the Superbowl, the CEO figures he has also heard a positive discussion about some aspect of Test Company's work.

In some ways, the soda machine has come to represent the quality of Test Company of which the CEO is most proud: its casual, flat, collaborative, organizational hierarchy. But this structure is not just the CEO's personal preference, it is by design. Test Company's customers pay a premium for the company's quick-turnaround manufacturing and delivery. Test Company's employees sometimes work late into the night to fulfill orders; on those nights, everyone pitches in to get the job done. Of the roughly 250,000 widgets the firm sells each year, half are sold at a 10 percent price premium. Instead of $25, Test Company can charge $27.50 for fast turnaround. The turnaround business accounts for $2.50 × 125,000 = $312,500 of extra revenue beyond normal delivery widgets. We assume no additional incremental costs, other than $1.00 of the incremental revenue paid out in overtime. The remaining $1.50 is incremental profit which translates into $187,000 per year.

Test Company's CEO is not sure how to attribute value directly to his firm's corporate culture, but he is willing to guess that without Test Company's cooperative efforts, the firm likely would lose at least half of its quick-turnaround business. Some quick math shows that incremental profit would fall by half to $93,500. The present value over the three-year period is:

$$\frac{\$93,500}{1.08} + \frac{\$93,500}{(1.08)^2} + \frac{\$93,500}{(1.08)^3} = \$241,000$$

Corporate culture and employee satisfaction seem to create Test Company's competitive advantage in the widget business. The CEO has even got a pretty good idea of what it is worth. But what about the soda machine?

The CEO knows that it is impossible to attribute a precise number to the economic benefit created by the soda machine in isolation. But he also knows that eliminating it will have some negative ramifications, which would need to be offset against the $34,000 Test Company would save from getting rid of it. So the CEO keeps on refining. He figures that the soda machine is probably one of the three most important social foci of Test Company, the other two being the company softball tournament and the annual holiday party. As a rough proxy, he sets up the following model:

Lost incremental profit without any corporate culture = $241,000

$241,000 = soda machine + softball game + holiday party+ unknowns

The CEO decides to test his model by assuming that the soda machine accounts for one-quarter of the value of the corporate culture of Test Company. This is about $60,000. If this is even close to reasonable, it appears that eliminating the soda machine (at a savings of $34,000) might do more harm than good.

DISCUSSION

Our highly stylized example of Test Company is, of course, designed to produce a compelling result. Although measuring inefficiencies seems within the normal bounds of management decision-making, valuing the soda machine's proto-asset income comes a lot closer to some fancy guesswork. Precision is difficult. Certainty is impossible. Even in Test Company's case, which was constructed to give a high value to the proto-asset, the CEO needs to know some important inputs—namely, that the firm would lose about half of its fast-turnaround business if employees were unable to pull together. Also, our CEO cannot be certain that "corporate culture" is the reason his employees are motivated during peak production times—they might do so simply out of fear of losing their jobs, or because of other fringe benefits. Soda suppliers would be happy to take credit for the benefit Test Company's employees derive.

The exercise of thinking through the cost-benefit analysis is much more valuable than placing a number on the soda machine. Test Company's CEO has a good idea of the total value of the organization's corporate culture (the $241,000); this exercise is just the first step in parsing that value out into the decisions the firm makes to invest in different assets.

We could imagine that the reason Test company's employees all pitch in at crunch time is because they *can*. Suppose that Test Company previously invested in a week of cross-training on all of the widget-manufacturing machinery; then the company's CEO might weigh the cost of that week's training against some part of the benefit he has calculated. Perhaps happy (and not thirsty!) employees count for only half of the value, and the net benefit of the cross-training investment accounts for the other half. As is obvious, each decision can seem to spiral in a myriad of cost-benefit equations. Good managers need to decide which ones are worth spending the time to understand. Our CEO might begin with corporate culture and the cross-training investment as two proto-assets, and then divide and subdivide the PIE-B several times to get a more accurate picture. With each subdivision, assumptions may be easier to make. Figure 6.1, on the following page, provides some variations on Test Company's PIE-B.

It is worth mentioning that these types of calculations are not simply hypothetical examples. The SAS Institute, a large statistical software firm located in North Carolina, provides its employees with many perks—a company golf course, swimming pools, on-site medical facilities, and even free dry-cleaning services. SAS's CEO, Jim Goodnight, is aware that offering such perks makes his employees more efficient and reduces turnover. Indeed, Stanford University's Jeffrey Pfeffer estimates that SAS's far lower turnover rate—3 percent versus 20 percent for other software firms—saves the company at least $60 million to $80 million per year in recruitment and training costs.[2]

Sprint is another example. The company recently designed its corporate headquarters with slow elevators and long distances between buildings in an effort to inculcate habits of exercise and thereby reduce healthcare costs. Union Pacific recently began a study to reduce obesity at the company, estimating that a 10 percent reduction in injury claims and illness expenses alone would save almost $17 million.[3]

If Test Company were up for sale, and we needed to value it, this text would not advocate adding $60,000 of soda machine proto-asset to the balance sheet. Even the broader allocation of $241,000 of potential lost profits to all the corporate culture or half of that to cross-training employees would be a tough sell to any auditor. It certainly is not in accordance with generally accepted accounting principles. What we should do is place these proto-assets in the PIE-B of Test Company in order to help understand any allocation of goodwill.

INCOME APPROACH AND INTANGIBLES

What is special about applying the income method to an intangible asset project? Several features can make the exercise challenging. First and most important, it may be very difficult to come up with reasonable and unbiased expected future cash flows. Put another way, the difficulty we have in identifying the intangible also makes it difficult to identify the good or bad outcomes that result in larger or smaller cash flows. Or the outcomes could be easy to identify, but it may be hard to assign them probabilities. There may be no preexisting market, or there may be features of at first seemingly

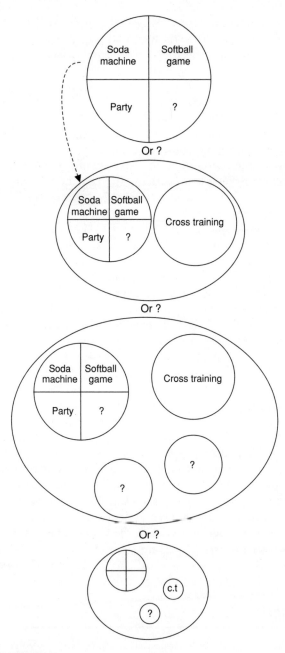

FIGURE 6.1 Test Company's PIE-B.

similar intangible assets and their associated cash flows that really differentiate them from the one under consideration.

Second, the project risk for the intangible asset may be significantly different from the company's overall risk. A discount rate that is appropriate for the firm as a whole may be wrong for an intangible asset of the firm. Ford Motors has a large intellectual property portfolio. The company controls thousands of patents and copyrights. Suppose that Ford was interested in licensing its "Mustang" trademark to an online gaming site. What discount rate should apply? Something more appropriate to use than the cost of capital in the automobile industry would be the capital cost for Internet services businesses, or perhaps the cost in the gaming industry. Those industries, in turn, have a different risk relationship to the market from the auto industry.

Third, if we were using a model like the CAPM to predict the riskiness of an intangible asset, it may be difficult to calculate beta. The existence of pure–play technology companies establishes some basis for using CAPM to determine intangible discount rates. But, much of the confidence we have in assigning an intangible asset beta has a lot to do with how much data we have. For example, record companies have a wealth of information about how record sales fluctuate with changes in the economy. If we were estimating future record sales for a hitherto unsigned artist, an asset beta derived from the past sales of reasonably similar artists may be just fine (although we need a definition of "reasonably similar" that is economically justified). What would not be fine is a blanket projection of future sales based only on the project-specific (artist-specific) risk.

Another peculiar feature of intangible assets is that their riskiness often changes over time. Their riskiness relative to the overall market may not change—that is, their discount rate should not change much—but their company-specific risk can vary wildly in successive periods. There can be a lot of reasons for this fluctuation, but some that come to mind are changes in the demand of the underlying asset—say, the popularity of a particular movie or recording star—or changes in demand for certain rapidly changing technologies. Compact disc sales in the United States for example, are reported to be down nearly 15 percent since the start of 2003, in part as a result of legal online music download services, illegal file-swapping networks, and increased digital piracy.[4]

OPTIONS MODEL

There is another tool we might consider using to help us with the fact that intangibles frequently change value over time: an option pricing model.

After all, nearly every day we hear about some sports team picking up a player's option. Are the fruits of that player's labor not intangible assets? Similarly, we read about a studio's option to make a sequel, or to use a particular actor, or to release a film for television. Does *option* mean the same thing in all these cases?

An option pricing model can be helpful when there is value associated with waiting to make some investment decision. The model also is helpful when investing in the asset has limited downside risk but unlimited upside potential. A financial option is thought of as an instrument that gives its holder the right, but not the obligation, to some future action. Usually it is the right to either buy or sell an asset. Let us think only of a *call option*, the right to buy something. Let us also consider only what is called a *European call option*, which is the type that can be exercised on only one date, the date of expiration.[5]

What is interesting for our purposes is that option pricing theory takes into account how the value of that right changes over time. A fundamental difference from calculating value based only on discounted cash flows is that the options model—which in the context of corporate decisions is called a *real option*—also takes into account the value of the ability to defer some investment decision. For intangibles, this comes up a lot. The decisions when to commercialize a patent, when to license a trademark, when to pick up the rights to a sequel, are all examples of option-like thinking.

Example: The Baseball Player's Contract

Let us think about a baseball player's contract. Suppose the team owner is willing to pay $1 million for the first year of a new player's contract, and also wants the option of signing him up for another year, at the end of the first season. The owner does not want to pay the player for a two-year contract because he is still unproven in the majors. The team's financial advisor decides to value the player's contract in this way: He calculates what they will have to pay the player in year 2; then he calculates what the player is likely to return in terms of extra ticket sales in that year.

The team will pay the player $1 million the first year and then the probability-weighted salary for the second year of a home-run king ($5 million), an average player ($1 million), and a player with a career-ending injury (0). The respective probabilities of each scenario are 30 percent, 60 percent, and 10 percent. The present value of the second-year salary is discounted at the risk-free rate of 5 percent. (It is discounted only one period

TABLE 6.1 Expected Sales

Sales	Probability	Expected
6.0	0.3	1.8
1.2	0.6	0.72
0	0.1	0
		2.52

Discounting rate of 5% gives $2.4 million.

because the re-signing occurs right after the first year.) The advisor's calculations for the cost of acquiring this player are:

$$\$1 \text{ million first year} + (.3 \times \$5 \text{ mil}) + (.6 \times \$1 \text{ mil}) + (.1 \times \$0)$$
$$= 1 + (1.5 + .6 + 0) = 1 + (2.1)/1.05 = 1 + 2 = \$3 \text{ million}$$

Because the owner already has decided to sign the player up for the first year, the cost of paying $2 million now for the second year is what really matters.

The value this player produces, which is the profit attributable to him through increased ticket sales, is estimated as 20 percent more than his salary. Obviously, if he turns out to be a home-run slugger, the team's return will be much greater than if he is just average, or worse yet, should he wind up injured. So, sales given the three possible outcomes are: $6 million as a home run slugger, $1.2 million as an average player, and 0 if he is injured. The value of the "investment" in the second year is $2.4 million, which is simply the expected $2.52 million discounted one period. Table 6.1 shows this calculation.

The net present value of signing this player for the second year is then $400,000: $2.4 million less $2 million now. This does not sound like enough to the owner. Is there some other calculation the owner can use?

Real Options Calculation

This is where we might consider a real options valuation to quantify waiting to sign the player for the second year. The real option on this player requires the same five inputs that are necessary to value a financial option. They are:

1. The value of the underlying asset (S), which is the expected year 2 value of $2.52 million

2. The variance *V* in the value of that asset, which is 0.82
3. The exercise price (*X*), which is the expected salary cost of $2.1 million
4. Time to expiration, or time until the decision can be deferred (1 year)
5. Riskless rate of return (5%)

We need to calculate the variance of the expected sales value of $2.52 million. In options language, what we want is the volatility associated with the different scenarios of this player's success in the second year. Using the expected probabilities is likely our best source; it is based on the comparable historical volatility of the team's other second-year players. Table 6.2 shows this calculation.

There are a couple of different ways to model this information, but the most widely used is probably the Black-Scholes options pricing model.[6] The details of how it works are beyond the scope of this text. Suffice to say that it was worthy of the 1997 Nobel Prize in economics.[7] Given some reasonable assumptions, we find that the option of waiting to sign this player up for his second year is worth about $1 million. The time premium of $600,000 is the difference between acting now, which is worth $400,000, and waiting, which is worth $1 million. This tells us that the team owner has up to that amount to negotiate as a signing bonus. For example, he can pay the player for the first year and also offer him $500,000 extra for the option to sign him for the next year. Even that would make the owner $100,000 better off than if he committed now to signing the player for year 2.

This example shows that when there is value in waiting to make decisions—as there often is with the changing quality of intangibles—an options pricing model is worth considering. To the pharmaceutical company CEO, the option on the baseball player's prospects in year 2 probably sounds a lot like an option on a new drug after it reaches Stage 3 Food and Drug Administration approval. In turn, those scenarios probably sound pretty familiar to movie studio executives who are trying to decide whether they want to buy the rights to make the sequel to next summer's potential action blockbuster.

TABLE 6.2   Option Calculation

Expected Salary Cost Year 2	Sales	Probability	Expected Sales	Mean	Variance	Standard Deviations
2.1	6.0	0.3	1.8			
2.1	1.2	0.6	0.72	0.84	0.8208	0.90598
2.1	0	0.1	0			
			2.52			

SUMMARY

In this chapter we learned about the basics of the income approach to valuation. It relies on calculating discounted cash flows, so we examined how to calculate present value. We then applied the income approach to value soda revenues, the cost of worker inefficiencies, and the value associated with Test Company's proto-asset: its corporate culture. We then thought about what contributed to corporate culture and hypothesized that some of it was represented by the soda machine. For Test Company's CEO, removing the machine became a more complicated decision once he could identify that it added something positive along both dimensions of the PIE-B. We also examined the idea of using an options methodology to value intangibles. Real options valuation helps address one of the frequent characteristics of intangible assets, namely their unpredictable cash flow outcomes. It also helps when there might be value in waiting to exercise the option.

APPENDIX

This appendix provides additional information about several of the factors we needed to calculate the discount rate based on the capital assets pricing model. Recall that the formula for the CAPM is:

$$r_i = r_f + \beta_i \times (r_m - r_f)$$

rf: The Risk-Free Rate

The *risk-free rate* represents the interest that could be earned by Test Company it were to place the cash flows associated with the soda sales in a safe investment, something like government Treasury bills or certificates of deposit. We assumed that rate was 2 percent. Typically, the risk-free rate incorporates a market forecast of inflation, but any analyst should be aware of the inclusion.

In our example, we were concerned only with predicting Test Company's soda revenues three years into the future. Inflation probably is not going to make a dollar in year 3 worth a whole lot less than one today. But as we noted earlier, sometimes we predict cash flows far out into the future: 20 years or more. In these models inflation makes a big difference. Would you be satisfied making your current income in, say, 1984 dollars? Probably not. There has been an 82 percent rate of price inflation over the last 20 years. According to the Federal Reserve, annual inflation currently is running at about 2.5 percent. In practice, a direct measure of inflation is rarely employed; it is implicitly embedded in our model assumptions. The important message here is that cash flows that are stated in nominal currency will need to be inflation adjusted. Likewise, cash flows expressed in real currency should not then be further discounted by inflation.

Diversifiable Risk

The next factor to analyze is *diversifiable risk*, also called the *project-specific risk*. In our example, the CEO has assumed that the cash flows that come from sales of soda are a sure thing. But suppose for a moment that is not so. Let us pretend that there is a 20 percent chance each year that Test Company's employees cut their soda consumption in half. (There is no national trend here, it is a feature peculiar to Test Company's employees.) Then cash flows from the soda machine would look like:

$$(.2 \times 1250 + .8 \times 2500) \times 3 = \$6{,}750$$

It is crucial to understand that this adjustment for risk associated with the "project" is made to the expected cash flows. This probability adjustment is far superior simply to raising the discount rate arbitrarily to lower the value. In many valuations, cash flows are projected at some steady growth rate. A good analyst asks whether the growth rate already takes into account the possibility of bad outcomes, or whether the valuation relies on an adjusted discount rate to arrive at a reasonable value. Readers should be wary of such adjustments—they almost always reflect a misunderstanding of the distinction between risks that are shared by the project and those that are systematic, or market-wide. To sum up: Diversifiable risk is not in the discount rate.

r_M: Required Market Return and Systematic Risk

Systematic risk is also called *market risk*. Think of this as big-picture risk that cannot be avoided or minimized by diversification by Test Company or any other business. The risk of macroeconomic trends, war, and cyclical swings in the economy are these types of risks. We assumed that required market return to compensate for these unavoidable types of risk was 8 percent. The *risk premium on the market* is simply the required market return less the risk free rate. So the market premium in our example was $8 - 2 = 6$.

Beta

One more term influences the risk premium on the market; this is the amount by which our project, our company, or our industry varies with the market. We assumed earlier that our soda cash flows varied the same as the market. That is, we assumed a *beta* of 1. But betas can range significantly; betas for security and commodities brokerages approach 3, while betas for petroleum firms are below 0.5. Suppose that we believed expected cash flows from the soda asset were 50 percent more volatile than the risk premium on the market. This would imply a beta of 1.5. The risk premium on the market would then be $1.5 \times (8 - 2)$, which is 9. Adding back the risk-free rate would result in a discount rate of 11.

CHAPTER 7

Market Approach and Intangibles

INTRODUCTION TO THE MARKET APPROACH

The second approach to valuation is the market method. The idea is that the value of an asset can be related to the value of comparable assets priced in the marketplace. For this reason the market approach sometimes is referred to as the comparables method. The trick for intangibles is defining the word "comparable." The more heterogeneous assets are, the more difficult it is to use the market approach. Another challenge is finding the "market." Put bluntly, there is not one for most intangibles.

This chapter covers the basics of the market approach; we work through an example of a patent intangible that is identifiable and separable, as well as an example of intangibles that cannot be separated. Our analysis also considers intangibles at public firms. This chapter introduces the economic concept of elasticity and the frequently used concept of market multiples.

SOME FEATURES OF THE MARKET APPROACH

If heterogeneous assets are hard to price using comparables, the reverse is also true. The market approach works better for commodities, or for assets whose attributes are easily delineated and are themselves easy to compare in a market that is actively traded. Pork bellies or bushels of corn are classic tangible examples. Real estate can also provide insight. When one is trying to determine the market value of a two-bedroom, new- construction condominium in downtown Chicago, there are literally thousands of like properties. Even if those did not exist, there are thousands of one- and three-bedroom examples to bracket the value of the two-bedroom unit. In other words, the similarity of location, square footage, and construction materials allows us to model the price of a two-bedroom unit with a fair amount of confidence.

Interestingly, the market approach usually is linked to other valuation principles. Prices at which the comparables are trading should take into account expected future cash flows. Because of this reliance on future cash flows, we scrutinize those underlying valuation assumptions as well. But a departure from other valuation ideas is that comparables give us an idea of *relative value*. The market approach is a benchmarking process with the implicit assumption that the comparables are priced correctly. If they have been systematically undervalued or overvalued (e.g., as were many Internet stocks in the late 1990s), so, too, will be the subject asset.

Another important point to remember is that what we observe in terms of prices of comparables is often the price of the commercialized embodiment of the intangible, not the underlying intangible itself. As we shall discuss, the demand for the intangible asset is not the same as the demand for the product that makes use of it.

Also, the distinction between stand-alone intangibles and intangibles that are inextricably linked to a firm relates to the same separability criteria the accounting rules make. With the patent, we may be able to isolate some traded prices for comparable patents. If we are attempting to value something inseparable, such as firm know-how, we will need to compare whole businesses. This does not mean that identifiable intangibles necessarily can be valued apart from the businesses that create them, only that unidentifiables rarely can.

Framing the Comparables Analysis

Let us start with a patent example. Suppose that we wish to value the patent for a pharmaceutical company's asthma medication designed for children. For now assume that there is no generic equivalent. A good comparables analysis takes into account asset prices at different depths and scope of similarity. Figure 7.1 represents one approach. It depicts these levels:

- All pharmaceutical patents
- Just asthma medication patents
- Just juvenile drug patents
- Just juvenile asthma drug patents

At first blush we might be tempted to use recent transactions prices (if they exist) for the category with the narrowest market definition, juvenile asthma drug patents. Recent patent sales might establish our starting point. Our next step is to ask why someone would pay more (or less) for our

All Pharmaceutical Patents

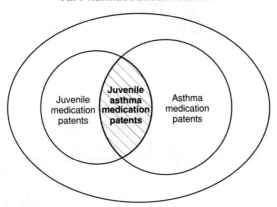

Juvenile medication patents

Juvenile asthma medication patents

Asthma medication patents

FIGURE 7.1 Example of Depth and Scope of Comparables.

patent than for one of the recently sold comparables? Here are five good reasons to start:

1. Fit, extension, or context
2. History
3. Scope
4. Useful remaining life
5. Likelihood of infringement

It could be that the comparable patent benefited the existing portfolio of the buyer in some way that our patent would not. Suppose that pharmacies prefer streamlining their buying from a limited number of sales representatives. It is easy to imagine that the comparable patent was the missing piece for whoever bought it. The buyer may have been willing to pay a premium to complete their portfolio of offerings to pharmacies—a premium that would not be reflected in the price of our patent. In other words, *the context matters*. Here it is an economy of scope.

The same asset might not be a close substitute for two different firms. An asthma medication patent may be worth about the same to Pfizer and Merck, but it may not present the same opportunities for a Baxter. Another possibility is that the price we are able to observe on the sale of a supposed comparable does not represent an arm's-length negotiation.

Now let us suppose that the comparable patent was derived from an adult asthma formula. When this patent was sold, the buyer knew that the consumer, the drug's manufacturer, the medical community, and the Food and Drug Administration already had some experience with the formula. Comparatively, our as-yet-untried patent is less valuable. However, we might imagine that our long track record for developing successful products is better than the record of the firm that owned the comparable patent. This may make our patent more valuable than the comparable. *History* probably tells us something (good or bad) about likelihood of success in the future.

It may be that the scope of the comparable patent is narrower (or broader) than our patent. Pretend the other patent can be used only in drug formulations for juvenile asthma; ours has proven beneficial in tests for arthritis as well. This wider *scope* most likely increases the value of our patent.

One of the patents may have a longer *useful remaining life* (which does not necessarily mean years left on patent). We might imagine that for the comparable patent, competitors have already filed their ANDAs (abbreviated new drug applications) and are waiting in the wings ready to introduce generic equivalents. Our patent, which may even have fewer years of protection left, might have no reasonable substitutes in the foreseeable future.

It could be the case that either our patent or the comparable patent is more *likely to be infringed*. One of the patents may be more poorly written, or one may be in a market that is more attractive to a potential infringer. It also could be the case that one drug manufacturer presents a more credible threat in case of a lawsuit. Another way to measure this criteria is along a dimension of ownership. Ownership, along with the economic benefits being owned, takes us back to the PIE-B.

These are just some reasons that the price for a comparable might not reflect accurately on the price we should expect for our intangible. Other lines of delineation focus on supply factors, such as similarities in production processes and the use of raw material.

As readers may be able to tell, this discussion is related to a definition of the market or industry in which we find ourselves. Economists wrestle mightily with market definition, as the task is rarely easy. We will discuss it more in Chapter 9.

PIE-B Applied to Comparables

From our discussion of the PIE-B in Chapter 5, readers know that the two dimensions for measuring the value of an intangible are ownership and amount of economic benefit. We also can think about comparables in these terms.

For a change of pace, let us pretend that the asset in question is a trade secret. Where along the spectrum of ownership would we place it? A truly comparable trade secret either would need to be in the same place along the

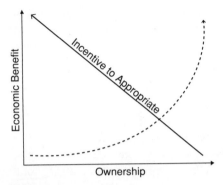

FIGURE 7.2   PIE-B and the Incentive to Appropriate an Intangible Asset.

two dimensions, or we would have to adjust along one or both dimensions to reflect an equivalent value. For instance, Coca-Cola's grip on the trade secret that is its formula for Coke is a lot firmer, than, say, my recipe for barbeque sauce. Coca-Cola has shown in the past its willingness to vigorously defend the secret. I have not spent much effort to protect my secret sauce formula.

But it is not just the legal muscle that Coke would employ to challenge a theft. It is the complexity of the recipe that ensures the firm's ability to deter stealing. In other words, the Coke recipe is harder to reverse-engineer. But consumer demand for the secret recipe is highly rewarded—much more so than for my barbeque sauce recipe. Therefore, the very fact that the secret is valuable might contribute to an increase in the possibility of discovery, since it will look attractive to other soda manufacturers. This would actually be a countervailing reduction in Coke's grip.

A better comparable for Coke than my secret barbeque sauce formula would be McDonald's recipe for French fries or Colonel Sanders' secret spices recipe. Figure 7.2 shows the incentive to appropriate an intangible asset, overlaid on the PIE-B's critical dimensions. The greater the economic benefit and the weaker the ownership, then the greater the incentive to appropriate.

ELASTICITY: A USEFUL ECONOMIC CONCEPT

The idea of comparability, the delineation along a spectrum of similarity or likeness, is at the heart of the economic concept of substitutes. Substitutability begins with a measurement of how intensely consumers demand a particular good. If there is sufficient data on sales, an economist might decide to quantify the demand for a good by undertaking a study of the price elasticity. The *price elasticity of demand* measures how much the quantity demanded of some good responds to changes in the price of that good. The equation is written as:

$$\text{Elasticity of demand} = \frac{\text{percentage change in quantity demanded}}{\text{percentage change in price}}$$

The elasticity is a negative number because, with a reduction in price, quantity normally moves in the opposite direction. (The reverse is true as well.) If, for example, the price of the patented drug at issue was reduced by 10 percent, from $100 to $90, and the quantity sold increased by 5 percent, from 100 units to 105 units, then the elasticity would be −0.5.

A small elasticity (usually measured relative to −1) means that a good is relatively inelastic—that is, its demanders are not particularly sensitive to changes in price. In life-and-death matters, for instance, we are generally inelastic to how much treatment costs; a cure for cancer would have a pretty small measure of elasticity. A large elasticity is just the opposite, when demanders are very sensitive to even slight changes in price. Soda could be an example of a relatively elastic good if one is standing in the soft drinks aisle in the supermarket, but it is very probably highly inelastic if one is on a deserted beach in 100-degree weather when a soda vendor suddenly appears. Again, context matters, because one's thirst varies.

The elasticity number is represented visually as the slope of the *demand curve*. The demand curve is nothing more than a plot of quantity versus price. Figure 7.3 shows two demand curves for soda under differing condi-

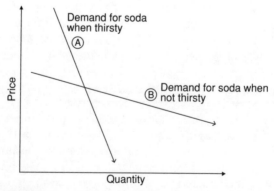

FIGURE 7.3   Elasticity of Demand for Soda.

tions. Line A depicts a steep (small) elasticity. Line B shows a nearly horizontal (large) elasticity.

Elasticity and Market Definition

Elasticity depends critically on how we define the market for substitutes. Although we will explore this more in Chapter 9, it is worth mentioning here. The broader we consider a product market, the more likely there are available substitutes, and the more elastic demand will be. If we are interested in measuring the demand for whole milk in a market defined as milk products, then we will consider as typical substitutes 2 percent, skim milk, half and half, and perhaps infant formula. If we are interested in measuring the demand for whole milk in the market of all beverages, we have many more substitutes to consider. The availability of substitutes tends to increase elasticity.

While intangible assets often have unique properties (remember why ten bad performances do not equal one great one?), they, too, are inelastically demanded the more unique they are—that is, the fewer the close substitutes. A generic lounge singer cannot command the same income as a Frank Sinatra or a Sarah Vaughn.

Elasticity and Time

Another feature is that demand often becomes more elastic over time. This fact is true because as consumers of a good are allowed time to search out alternative substitutes in response to a price increase, they become more elastic in their demand for the original. Also, given more time, manufacturers are more likely to be able to devise substitutes that create the opportunity for more elastic demand. (This is supply elasticity, which we cover later.)

Cross-Price Elasticity

Now that we have covered the basics, we can extend this concept into a measurement of how much two goods are substitutes for each other. The concept of substitutes is frequently measured numerically by the *cross-price elasticity of demand* (CPEoD) for the two goods under consideration. Its formula is:

$$\text{CPEoD} = \frac{\Delta Q1}{\Delta P2}$$

where numerator = percentage unit change in the quantity of good 1
denominator = percentage unit change in the price of good 2

In the simple case, this benchmark is used:

CPEoD > 0, then the two goods are substitutes
CPEoD = 0, then the two goods are independent of each other
CPEoD < 0, then the two goods are complements

Prices for Intangibles versus the Underlying Goods

In practice, it is often difficult to get data rich enough to undertake a study of the elasticity of demand; and this is especially true in pricing intangibles. In the (likely) absence of recent prices for sales of patents in our hypothetical pharmaceutical example, we might look for historical data on price changes for the types of drugs covered by the patents we are testing as comparables, and see how volume or market share of the products changed in response. (Scanner data might be used for these purposes.) The cross-price elasticity helps us with the hypothesis that using these comparables in the market approach is reasonable, but we certainly need to recognize that quantity or price changes for reasons that have nothing to do with the direct demand for the intangible. *When we look at price data for the products that embody intangible assets, we are measuring the elasticity of demand for the products, not for the intangible assets themselves.*

Put another way, demand for the whole good is not the same as demand for the intangible assets that go into the good. One reason for this might be how much of the cost of the whole good is represented by the intangibles. If denture replacements cost $10,000, and $9,800 of that is labor, even a large change in the price of the denture materials—say a 50 percent change, from $200 to $300—will not deter most people who were already thinking about dentures from getting them.

Elasticity of Supply

The *price elasticity of supply* (PEoS) tells us how much the quantity of a good supplied changes in response to a change in price of that good. The formula is:

$$PEoS = \frac{\Delta Q}{\Delta P}$$

The more inelastic the supply is of some good, the less able the manufacturers of that good are able to respond. Suppose that the patent at issue is valuable because it can reduce the manufacturing time to test early-stage drug formulas. (In fact, this very technology helped launch Millennium Pharmaceuticals.) If a patent covers an input that can be supplied easily outside of the patent—in other words, by designing around the patent—then the patent is worth less than the alternative in which the patented method or product is the only way to get the good. Put another way, supply elasticity can depend on how costly it is for competitors to figure out another way to replace the invention described by the patent. (This should sound familiar; it is the engineer-around or opportunity cost construct again.) Holding all other factors constant, the more elastic the supply, the less valuable this patent would be.

Summary of Comparable Intangible Assets

The right comparables may not be at the narrowest market definition. Setting aside the fact that there may be little or no data available at that level, using our earlier example, it could be that markets price "juvenile" drug patents similarly, or "asthma" drug patents similarly, or perhaps all the patents developed by certain pharmaceutical firms warrant special consideration. There is no hard-and-fast rule for determining at what level to draw comparables, but a good valuation based on comparables needs to be justified by economic principles. We should endeavor to keep in mind the concept of elasticity when we think about comparables, and we should remember that the prices we observe are not necessarily prices for the intangible assets we wish to value; they can be prices of the inventions or products that make use of the intangibles. Most important, a comparables analysis that does not extend into the underlying economic factors like ownership and benefits should raise a red flag.

COMPARABLE FIRMS

So far our discussion here has been on comparable assets or the products that make use of those assets. But comparables analysis also is performed with respect to whole firms. How do we take into account intangibles that are not identifiable? First, we need to understand generally how comparable firms are analyzed. Let us begin with publicly traded companies.

When firms are publicly traded, there is usually a price available every day. The stock price is the market's estimate of what equity in the firm is worth. The market helps us place a value on the bundle of all the assets of the firm, tangible and intangible. We still may have to model the pieces of the intangible component using other methods, but public firms at least avoid the problem of there being "no market." Public firms often are analyzed through the use of *market multiples*. Because of the availability of frequent prices, as well as the often-voluminous reporting requirements, public firms are frequently used to benchmark private firms. Accounting ratios also are used to compare values across public and private companies.

Market Multiples

Market multiples present a way to standardize a comparables analysis. As the name implies, they are measurements that are multiples of *something*; that something usually is an accounting construct. Earnings and revenues are the accounting measurements that typically are used in multiples analysis. We might say that a firm is "trading at five times EBITDA" or has "10X on revenues." This means that the stock price is equal to five times the firm's EBITDA, or annual earnings before interest, taxes, depreciation, and amortization. The phrase "10X on revenues" means that the stock price is equal to 10 times the annual revenues of the firm. Or, in the case of private firms, it may mean that firms recently have been acquired for an amount 10 times revenues.

The market multiple implicitly considers that the firm will be able to generate the accounting measurement being used for some amount of time in the future. If readers think that this sounds something akin to the present value of the future cash flows, they would be correct.

Efficient Investing   So what do market multiples have to do with comparables analysis? The logic is that investors price comparable firms at comparable multiples. Analysts and investment bankers like to use multiples as a shorthand method for standardizing the earnings power or growth power of a firm. The ratio of a dollar of stock price to x dollars of earnings then can be compared not just across comparables within an industry, but across the whole market. If the price of Company A's stock is $100 per share, and it earns $1 per share, the multiple is 100X earnings. If Company B has a stock price of $20 per share, and it earns $0.20 per share, it, too, has a 100X earnings multiple. From the investor's standpoint, all else equal, the value (at least according to this one metric) of these firms is the same.

In addition, multiples analysis is helpful for performing a gut check across supposedly comparable firms. If we know that the current stock price for widget makers is between 7 and 10 times their pretax earnings, it might be unreasonable for us to claim that the stock price for a widget-making firm we wish to buy is overpriced and should be closer to 2 times earnings. We can draw this conclusion based in part on the information efficiency in open markets: The owners of the firm we wish to purchase would respond that it is pretty unlikely we know better what the firm is really worth—there can be little private information left that would account for the large discrepancy.

Private Values from Public Counterparts   Multiples also are used frequently to compare private firms with their public counterparts. If they are all making the same product, the theory goes, then the private firm's equity (which is not publicly traded) should be priced like its public cousins' stocks. But an important distinction to draw is the difference between a measurement of the equity and a measurement of the enterprise value. Enterprise value is defined as the total amount of investment in the firm—equity and debt (which is calculated as market capitalization plus debt and preferred shares, minus cash and cash equivalents). The prices we observe for public firms are what the firms are worth to shareholders. In a comparables analysis that attempts to price a private firm against a public one, we have to remember that the purchasers of the private firm also are taking over any debt. Without accounting for debt in the private firm, we would overvalue it based solely on the equity of a publicly traded comparable. In addition, there can be a public-to-private *liquidity discount* employed to reflect the fact that equity in the private firm is (as the name implies) less liquid.

Fair Value and Premiums   The Financial Accounting Standards Board prescribes fair value for measuring the worth of intangibles. Because the fair value represents the market price at which two parties negotiating in good faith would arrive, it is closely related to market value. However, we need to be careful not to interpret the market capitalization of a publicly traded firm as equivalent to the fair value of the assets. One reason is because the market price can, especially when an acquisition is being contemplated, reflect various premiums or discounts.

An acquirer may pay a *control premium*, for example, if by taking over the firm it will gain not just in size, but in managerial control of the now-larger combined entity. In other words, it pays to be in the driver's seat. There are (in theory) anticipated cost savings or synergies that will result from one set of managers where there used to be two. Alternatively, acquisition prices may reflect a *minority discount* (when the value of shares is discounted because there are not enough shareholders to affect managerial control).

In the goodwill impairment testing required by Financial Accounting Standard 142, it is important to consider whether it is even appropriate to allocate any control premium to a reporting unit. Suppose that the cash flows of the reporting unit have been forecasted using the income approach, and they already internalize synergies or cost savings that would be reflected by the control premium. Then no control premium is necessary; it is already "built in" to the cash flows of the reporting unit. In this view, the control premium is not some bodiless intangible asset tacked on to the goodwill in an acquisition. Rather, it reflects some of the anticipated economic benefits that will result from combining the entities.[1]

Avoiding Some Pitfalls

As popular as multiples are, they are misused very often, and that misuse can be exacerbated in firms with a large number of intangible assets. To begin with, it is essential to know what is captured in the accounting measurement that is part of the multiple. "Earnings" is defined as a lot of different things: gross income; operating income; net income; earnings before interest and taxes (EBIT); and earnings before interest, taxes, depreciation, and amortization (EBITDA). It might be defined as 12-month trailing earnings, average annual earnings, or quarterly earnings. If these are different—or not knowable—for firms in the comparables analysis, the resulting multiples are likely to be, at the very least, inaccurate.

Novice and experienced valuation analysts alike frequently ask: What multiple should I use? There is no one best multiple. Each measure of earnings, revenues, or return on investment sheds different light on what is comparable across firms. For this reason, it is important to test what a multiple does *not* reveal. For example, periodic statements may obscure the trends in a highly seasonal business; statements that span longer periods may be key to understanding a firm's profitability or projections. Or suppose that returns play an important role in a particular industry (as they do in the book business—although I hope not in books on this subject). Then a comparison of gross sales would be misleading; net sales would be more appropriate.

Moreover, price multiples do not have to tell us anything about the amount of debt at comparable firms. A highly levered company can have a much better-looking EBITDA price multiple than a firm less reliant on debt, for example. Does this mean that that firm is worth more? No. It means that debt is more important to one. That may or may not matter to us, but we better know if we are about to make some valuation judgment using the EBITDA multiple.

Even knowing that the accounting terms are defined the same across firms or within industries is not necessarily enough to rest comfortably with our choice of a multiple. Firms within the same industries (to say nothing about across industries) have a fair amount of discretion in how they assign costs and how much they treat as fixed and variable. Multiples cannot tell us, for example, how each firm allocates labor costs. All things being equal, a firm that has some discretion to capitalize more sales labor as part of the cost of goods sold will have a lower gross margin than an identical firm that expenses sales labor. This type of concern is warranted particularly when comparing the audited financial statements of public firms to, say, the compiled statements of private peers.

Some Statistical Issues

Selection bias and the standard deviation are two statistical concepts to bear in mind when thinking about a list of comparables and the data (financial ratios or other) that we take from them.

Selection Bias   Suppose that we are interested in comparing a financial measurement for our subject company with the measurement in a set of comparable firms. What can we say statistically about the measurement we wish to examine?

First we need to understand statistically how the peers were selected. Do they represent the population of all comparables, or are the peers a sample? If they are a sample, then we need to be sure the sample was randomly drawn from the larger population. Even a very large sample will not be representative if there is selection bias. In addition, in statistics there is something called *nonresponse bias*. In our example this would be the equivalent of missing data. Firms with no data to report—say, negative price-to-earnings ratios—could be different in other significant ways from the population. If the comparables really are selected from a sample, the best sampling method introduces no bias—it is simple random sampling (sometimes called a probability method).

In practical terms, a valuation analyst rarely may have to worry about sampling a large population of peers. But selection bias creeps in even in small numbers. When valuations throw out companies and their data —perhaps because they are "too big" or "too small" or "too new"—we have to think hard about the underlying economic justifications. This circles back to our earlier discussion of analyzing the depth and scope of comparables.

Standard Deviation   Suppose that we are comfortable with our peer selection. Maybe we have been able to collect data for the whole population of peers, so there is no sampling issue. We need to take special note when valuations make uninformed reference to the average value of some comparables' measurement without knowing what the standard deviation is. The standard deviation tells us how far away from the average the numbers on a list are. Although the formula may look intimidating,

$$\sigma_l = \sqrt{\frac{\sum_{i=1}^{N} d_i^2}{N-1}}$$

it is relatively painless to calculate in six steps.

1. Calculate the mean of the numbers ($i = 1$ through N).
2. Take the difference each number on the list is from the mean (d).
3. Take the square of all the differences.
4. Add up all those squared differences.
5. Take the average of the squared differences (which is sometimes corrected for smaller lists by reducing the number of items on the list by 1, hence $N - 1$)
6. Take the square root of that average.

Suppose that a financial ratio we believe is important to use for comparison returns an average value of 5 for the peer group, with a standard deviation of 0.5. Our ability to say that 5 is a meaningful benchmark for the ratio for our firm is much better (holding everything else constant) than if the average ratio was 5 and the standard deviation was 3. We should then ask: What accounts for the wide swing away from the average in the second measurement? And how wide is too wide? In other words, maybe the peers in the second group are not as comparable as we thought.

Our ability to make statements about how good the estimate is depends in part on whether the data are normally distributed. In a normal distribution, most (about 95 percent) of the values should lie within two standard deviations of the average. Whether most financial ratios are normally distributed is an entirely different issue and significantly beyond the scope of this book. (In general, they are not thought to be.) The purpose here is to simply raise readers' awareness.

Multiples and Intangibles

Intangible assets and multiples are frequently a volatile mix. As we saw in Chapter 3, the problems with multiples analysis can magnify because of the disconnect between accounting measurements and intangibles generally, and also because of the special characteristics of firms that invest heavily in intangibles. It is critical to be aware of these accounting and economic distinctions. Just the example of price-to-earnings (P/E) ratios makes this clear. Setting aside different definitions of earnings in the denominator, firms with a lot of intangibles sometimes exhibit extremely small or even negative earnings numbers. This situation can make P/E ratios either gargantuan or unusable. Whenever readers see a very large P/E ratio relative to some comparables, check to make sure that the earnings for the period are not unusually small. And if earnings are negative, then consider using the inverse of the P/E ratio, which is called the *earnings yield*. Although the statistical example just given does not reflect on intangibles per se, the rather uninformative results are fairly common when we try to price "comparable" firms with heavy intangible asset investments. The volatility of measurements across these types of firms should never be ignored.

UNIDENTIFIABLE INTANGIBLES AND COMPARABLES

So far in this chapter we have mostly analyzed identifiable intangible assets. Patents, trademarks, and copyrights are bought and sold. So are brands. But what about assets such as know-how, a highly trained executive team, or an exceptionally happy workforce? How can we use the comparables method to figure out those values?

By definition, these types of intangibles are inseparable from the firm. To calculate their value, we have two options. We can hope that there have been recent sales of comparable firms to the one that contains the unidentifiable asset we seek to value. But this assumes that either we can attribute all of the goodwill in the comparable sale to the same unidentified intangible, or we have some way of parsing out the proto-assets that comprise the goodwill. It assumes, also, that goodwill was created. So unless we have a method for prying out the unidentified asset, we will be reduced to guessing.

But there is another way to introduce the idea of comparables. We can introduce another valuation method to estimate the value of comparable unidentifiable assets *within* the firm. Suppose we assume that the reason one firm is more valuable than another is happier workers. An income model could rely on knowing the difference in productivity rates between an unhappy worker and a happy one. For argument's sake, we might assume that sick employees are a rough approximation for unhappy ones. We could examine the firm's employment records, calculating the average productivity of workers who were sick with those who were not.

Another calculation we might do is to compare a particularly sick worker's productivity with the average sick worker's. This calculation holds sickness constant and seeks to measure the reduced productivity of an extra sick worker. With either estimate, the difference in productivity over some period of time—*in other words, the difference in earnings from otherwise comparable workers*—would give us an estimate of the value of the intangible happiness proto-asset per worker.

Another way to measure unhappiness might be to consider striking workers. The total cost of labor unrest in the form of strikes or work slowdowns will be our proxy for unhappiness. Again, a firm that has happy workers avoids this cost, which is equal to the value of the happiness intangible. We might write the formula in this way:

Total Value of Happiness = (Number of Workers)
　　　　　　　　　　　× (likely length of a strike over time *t*)
　　　　　　　　　　　× (cost in lost productivity over *t*)
　　　　　　　　　　　× (expected probability of strike during *t*)

If some preliminary results using this model looks promising, then we will need to get more serious about happiness. Are strikers or sick workers really a good proxy for unhappy ones? In the language of economists, are they good instruments for the variable that we wish to measure (happiness) but cannot observe directly? An important characteristic of a good instrument is that it does not vary independently with the item we wish to measure. Could strikers or sick workers independently explain lower productivity (or sales) apart from happiness? At this point, some further statistical analysis, probably in the form of a regression, would be in order. If our feelings about the value of relative worker happiness were confirmed by surveys or employee interviews, we might think about including happiness as a proto-asset in the PIE-B. At the least, managers of the firm might think about provisioning for a strike or extra medical costs at a firm where workers are less happy.

SUMMARY

In this chapter we discussed some of the important concepts involved in the market approach to valuing intangibles. Fundamentally, the ideas are the same as applied to tangible assets: using other assets as benchmarks for an indication of value. With intangibles, we need to be especially concerned about what we have identified as the proto-asset. Elasticity is a useful concept to help us differentiate between goods, although we cannot always measure or even observe the underlying intangibles. Furthermore, we examined some of the reasons for using multiples and some of the pitfalls involved in assuming comparables are really appropriate. Last, we discussed the idea of using the income approach in conjunction with comparables in order to benchmark unidentifiable intangibles within a firm.

In the next chapter we examine the cost approach.

APPENDIX: SOURCES FOR COMPARABLES

So where do analysts find comparable public firms? There are several places. Analysts first should examine the target firm's own financial statements. Sometimes, either in the discussion of the business, or in the management, discussion, and analysis section of the Securities and Exchange Form 10-K, the firm makes explicit reference to its competitors. Then consider looking at firms with the same Standard Industrial Classification (SIC) code as the target. This classification system, which is now called the North American Industrial Classification System (NAICS) was created by the United States, Canada, and Mexico. It groups industries at different levels of comparability, using two- through six-digit classification codes, in increasingly narrower definitions of industries.

For example, Microsoft has several different two-digit classifications:

retail trade
information
management of companies and enterprises
manufacturing
professional, scientific, and technical services
wholesale trade

General Mills has only one two-digit classification: manufacturing. But both firms' businesses are further narrowed to five- or six-digit descriptions. Table 7.1 shows the hierarchy of Microsoft's information classification and General Mills' manufacturing classification.

In addition, industry analysts, trade press, and private data vendors are all possible sources for locating comparables.

TABLE 7.1   NAICS Classification

General Mills	Microsoft
31 - Manufacturing	51 - Information
311 - Food Manufacturing	511 - Publishing Industries (except Internet)
3112 - Grain and Oilseed Milling	5112 - Software Publishers
31123 - Breakfast Cereal Manufacturing	51121 - Software Publishers
311230 - Breakfast Cereal Manufacturing	511210 - Software Publishers

Source: U.S. Census Bureau NAICS Codes and Titles.
http://www.census.gov/epcd/naics02/naicod0.2.htm. International Directory of Company Histories 36 and 63. Ed. Jay P. Pederson (New York, NY: St. James Press, 2004) Vol 36 and 63.

CHAPTER 8

Cost Approach and Intangibles

The third approach we will consider is the cost method. This chapter explores the relationship between what an intangible asset costs and what that asset is worth. Like tangible assets, intangibles change in value over time. Sometimes they are worth more than they cost; other times they have depreciated in value. But unlike with tangibles, that depreciation is not straightforward because it is not physical. Intangibles "wear out" for other reasons, and unearthing that wear and tear requires economic analysis. It is critical to recognize that original or book cost may have little to do with the value of the intangible asset. When that is the case, one of the other two approaches usually is needed. This chapter examines original cost, book cost, and replacement cost.

ORIGINAL COST

The first cost to consider for a valuation is the original cost to acquire or make a particular asset. This is almost always the wrong number to use because assets increase or decrease in value over time (setting aside any effect of inflation). A collectible vintage car's original price is far lower than the price it can command in the market today. Yet few people would be willing to buy a used typewriter today for anywhere near its original cost.

The same possibilities exist for intangible assets. A copyright, for instance, may go up or down in value for reasons that have nothing to do with the cost to create the work. For intangibles, the original cost is likely to include a hefty labor component that (as we learned in Chapter 3) is incurred up front. Human capital is an ingredient to making anything, but it features prominently in intangibles. The cost to make a major motion picture may include enormous production expenditures on tangibles—sets, costumes, lighting, location, cameras—but the actors, directors, and crew also can be sizable expenses. Large pharmaceutical firms spend significantly to outfit their scientists' laboratories, but the cost of the scientists' salaries is substantial. Software firms obviously spend a lot of money on programmers—they are the most important raw material in producing software products. Intellectual property is intellectual for a reason.

BOOK COST

Book cost is whatever is recorded in a company's financial statements. As we learned in Chapter 4, the rules for amortizing and depreciating identifiable intangibles are designed to take into account some approximation of the remaining useful life of the intangibles. Other intangibles, such as goodwill, never depreciate, but are subject to the impairment tests we looked at earlier.

How well the booking assumptions match reality depends on the economic characteristics of the asset. For example, the assumption that book cost accurately reflects a pharmaceutical patent's worth might depend on some of these factors:

- Whether the patent has been incorporated into a new drug
- Where in the Food and Drug Administration (FDA) approval process the drug stands
- How the drug has been selling
- Where the competition and demand will be when the drug comes off patent
- How old the patent is

These factors help determine the patent's fair value, which in turn implies what the remaining useful life is. Notice that some of these factors (how the drug has been selling, where competition stands) require us to bring in the other two valuation methods. Sales and profits often are best measured using the income approach, and the competition might be measured using the market approach.

Suppose that the patented drug fails to pass Phase III FDA approval and therefore will never reach the consumer marketplace. If this happens, the drug's useful life is as good as over (at least for this intended purpose). The company that holds the patent will probably depreciate it very rapidly when this unfavorable news is disclosed, because now the asset is impaired.

REPLACEMENT COST

Replacement cost is the next concept to consider. It is also the most ambiguous because we must interpret the term "replacement." Should we value an exact replacement for an asset, or should we value one that imitates it?

Suppose a firm holds the patent on a certain kind of epoxy glue that bonds two surfaces to a prespecified tolerance in a set amount of time (say, under 10 seconds). The cost to come up with the patent for this epoxy was $100 million four years ago. That is the original cost. (We have assumed for simplification that there were no development costs before winning patent approval.) The patent has been depreciated on a straight-line basis, which puts the book cost at about $76.5 million. (This is simply $5.9 million of depreciation per year for four years. The annual amount is based on a 17-year life.) Now the firm has been involved in a lawsuit in which it alleges that another company has infringed the patent. The court has ruled that as a matter of damages, the owner is entitled to the current replacement cost.

Functional Equivalency and Design-Around Cost

With that instruction, one alternative to consider is the cost to develop a *functionally equivalent* substitute. Suppose that now an epoxy exists on the market that cost $80 million to develop, and it bonds at the same strength in 8 seconds. It also costs the consumer the same amount as the 10-second epoxy. Since this epoxy would be acceptable to users of the original 10-second epoxy, the replacement cost might be measured as the $80 million.

Alternatively, suppose that the only reasonably close epoxy substitute cost $120 million to develop and bonds in 12 seconds. Then the replacement cost is at least $120 million. In fact, that amount would undercompensate the original inventor if the 12-second epoxy was not valued identically by consumers. How much more it would cost to advance the epoxy technology (in order to reduce the bonding time another 2 seconds) would have to be added to the replacement cost to arrive at a value for the patent. Another way to measure this increment is to calculate the lost profit facing the firm that will lose some business as a result of the less-desirable 12-second bonding time.

The idea of replacement cost is often very close to the engineering concept of design-around cost. For example, how much would it cost to design around the patent for a certain type of rubber sole for athletic shoes? Or the patent on a folding pocket knife? Or a key-chain flashlight? If there is nothing particularly special about these patented designs, then noninfringing substitutes might cost little more than the effort to change a proportion here or there, or add slightly different ingredients to the invention's batter. The tweaks need to be great enough to escape infringing the patents, but not so great as to result in perceptibly inferior goods.

Special properties of these goods may make them highly valuable, in a way that minor tweaks to would-be infringers will not solve. In the language of economists, we would say that the supply for the special proper-

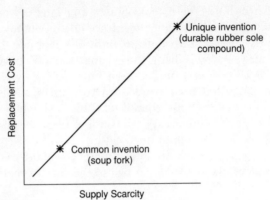

FIGURE 8.1   Soup Forks and Rubber Soles.

ties is relatively inelastic. Figure 8.1 shows this relationship between replacement cost (value) and supply scarcity (uniqueness).

Some athletic shoes with a proprietary durable rubber compound sole would be in the upper right area of the graph. A relatively worthless patent, say a business method patent for eating soup with a fork, lies in the lower left area. In our example, the demand for the products is correlated with the supply; the athletic shoes with the durable soles are popular, the soup-fork eating method is not. But this does not have to be the case—there certainly can be limited supply for something and limited demand, as well, or the reverse. Titanium-tipped shoelaces may be hard to come by, but there also may be no demand for them.

When Replacement Cost Means Lost Profits

But here is an important limiting distinction to draw. The concept of replacement cost can balloon in litigation to encompass far more than just the cost to develop an alternative asset. It also might include the success attributable to the asset in question. This extension of the meaning of replacement to include lost profits can be hefty. In a lawsuit, plaintiffs may claim that when their asset was misappropriated, they lost far more than the cost to replace the asset. But usually such "victims" have a duty to mitigate. In other words the "victims" cannot be damaged by more then the cost to find a substitute. Of course, sometimes there is no substitute, or at least, no cheap one. In that case, we should not jump to the conclusion that an extrapolation to lost profits is necessarily wrong—rather, we need to undertake a careful analysis of causation.

Replacement cost was featured prominently in the failed savings and loan crisis. In the early 1980s the federal government allowed some thrifts to take over other weaker thrifts in order to stave off rampant closures. One of the ways the federal government facilitated this was to allow the acquiring thrifts to count the weaker thrifts' negative net worth as a kind of asset, called supervisory goodwill. This was attractive to the acquirers because this new intangible could count toward meeting their regulatory requirements and, in effect, would allow them to lend more, which in turn could make the thrifts bigger and more profitable.

In 1989 Congress passed a law called the Financial Institutions Reform and Recovery Enforcement Act (FIRREA). One of the important provisions of this law was to remove thrifts' ability to count the supervisory goodwill toward their capital requirements. FIRREA required that the intangible asset would have to be amortized away rapidly. Some thrifts argued that this was unfair. They claimed that no longer being able to count supervisory goodwill would put them out of business, because the asset base against which they could make loans would shrink. All of a sudden, many of these thrifts were out of regulatory compliance. Indeed, in 1996 the courts found for the thrifts, making the government liable for breach of contract.

All told, more than 120 thrifts filed lawsuits. Experts for the thrifts claimed that the government was liable not just for removing the intangible asset, but for the damage that such removal caused.[1] Lost profits figured prominently in some of the earliest cases. The plaintiffs believed that the government needed to replace the success the thrifts would have had but for the breach caused by FIRREA. But, after lost profits calculations were found to be too speculative, the thrifts' experts concentrated on measuring the value of the lost supervisory goodwill by proxy. They postulated that the thrifts would need to replace the goodwill with some other asset in order to avoid shrinking or going out of business. In most of their models, the plaintiffs' experts replaced the supervisory goodwill with synthetic preferred stock, designed to replicate the characteristics of the goodwill.

The government's experts had a much stricter view of replacement cost. It did not mean replacing lost profits, and it did not even mean replacing the supervisory goodwill with a like amount of preferred stock. (According to the government, either replacement would surely overcompensate the thrifts, since what they lost was an accounting construct, and what they would gain under the plaintiffs' scenario was hard, cold cash.) Rather, the government argued that damages were limited to the transaction costs associated with replacing the goodwill. In other words, replacement cost was literally only the fees associated with raising new capital in the amount of the lost supervisory goodwill.[2]

Although the intangible in the case of the failing thrifts was a financial asset, it is instructive to see that it is the effort required to replace the asset—the transaction costs—that matters in determining how much the asset is worth. Transaction costs here are synonymous with design-around costs. If some asset is really costly to replace, it is obviously more valuable.

SUMMARY

Using an intangible asset's original cost for its value often misses the web of complementarities that give value to intangibles. Book cost relies on an economically sensible application of depreciation—something that usually cannot be done without referring to fair value, a concept that is frequently derived from the market or income approaches. And, as the preceding examples should have made clear, replacement cost has a range of interpretations. It can be as narrow as the transaction costs or friction created when replacing one asset with another, or as broad as meaning replacing the market success an asset has allowed its owners to achieve. In the next chapter we explore some additional legal aspects of intangibles.

CHAPTER 9

Intangible Assets and Litigation

In the last three chapters we explored how intangible assets can be valued using the three basic approaches: income, market, and cost. Many of the examples thus far have imagined the sale of assets or companies that are willingly engaged in a transaction. But a great deal of valuation occurs in the litigation arena, and many of these analyses take place under less-than-friendly circumstances. Patents are infringed, trade secrets are stolen, copyrights are violated, and trademarks are diluted. These conditions provide a rich framework for analyzing valuation. This chapter presents two important concepts as applied to identifiable intangibles: the *Panduit* test for lost profits and the *Georgia Pacific* factors for determining a reasonable royalty. In addition, we discuss what constitutes a trade secret, how to define dilution, and what makes a mark (legally) famous.

PANDUIT TEST

In 1964 the Panduit Corporation, a maker of wiring and communication products, brought a patent infringement case against Stahlin Bros. Fibre Works, Inc. Panduit alleged that Stahlin was infringing its patent covering the duct for wiring electrical control systems. The court ruled that the patent plaintiff, Panduit, was eligible to recover lost profits damages if the criteria of a four-pronged test were satisfied. These criteria are:

1. There is a demand for the patented product.
2. There are no acceptable noninfringing alternatives available in the marketplace.
3. The plaintiff had (or has) sufficient manufacturing and marketing capacity to be able to exploit the demand that would have existed in the absence of defendant's alleged infringement.

4. The patent plaintiff is able to determine with reasonable accuracy the amount of profit that it would have made in the absence of defendant's allegedly infringing sales.

In a patent infringement case, one or both sides may employ a valuation expert to examine the market and businesses involved to determine if the *Panduit* test is met. But even if there is no lawsuit under way, these criteria can help us determine how valuable the patent is.

For lawyers, the first criteria is straightforward: It is incumbent on the plaintiff's counsel to show that the patent is of some useful good that is currently being demanded in the marketplace. A patent on a tool is a good example. All that is necessary for the lawyer is to show that the tool is being sold in hardware stores. The patent "Method of Preserving the Dead" (No. 748,284, December 29, 1903) may be more problematic. There is little evidence that it is in use or will be in use in the marketplace.

The bar for valuation experts is higher. They need to know *how much* demand exists for the invention. This does not mean demand for the product that encompasses the patent, but rather demand for the patented feature itself. Suppose that a hammer is the product at issue, and the patent covers the design of a nonslip grip. What is important to know is not just the quantity and price of hammers, but the quantity and price of hammers with the patented nonslip grip, as well as information on other substitutes. This information tells us how much consumers value the incremental worth of the patent, rather than how much they value hammers.

This leads us to the second *Panduit* criteria, the presence or absence of acceptable noninfringing substitutes. For instance, is there another type of grip-improving handle that is affixed to hammers that does not infringe the nonslip patent? Are consumers indifferent to which kind of handle they have? Let us return to the concept of elasticity. Suppose the price of the patented grip hammer was raised 10 percent, and quantity purchased of the noninfringing substitute-grip hammer increased 5 percent. The cross-price elasticity of demand is 0.5, which indicates that the two might be substitutes. But this is only a start.

MARKET DEFINITION

The preceding analysis raises a critical question. How did we know what other goods to consider as substitutes? What if consumers switch to plain-vanilla hammers if the price of the patented grip hammer is increased? What if they switch to mallets or screwdrivers or electric staplers in response to a price increase? Or perhaps consumers would be willing simply to buy some sticky tape and wrap it around the grip instead.

Because the patent holder is a temporary monopolist, it may be illustrative to look at what the Horizontal Merger Guidelines (jointly issued by the U.S. Department of Justice and the Federal Trade Commission) say about defining the market in which a monopolist can profitably operate. Including or excluding products using the guidelines' market test can inform us about the availability of substitutes. It states:

> *A market is defined as a product or group of products and a geographical area in which it is produced or sold such that a hypothetical profit-maximizing firm, not subject to price regulation, that was the only present and future producer or seller of those products in that area likely would impose at least a "small but significant and nontransitory" increase in price, assuming the terms of sale of all other products are held constant. A relevant market is a group of products and a geographic area that is no bigger than necessary to satisfy this test.*[1]

In our example, could the hammer maker with the patented grip impose a "small but significant and nontransitory" increase in the price of its hammers that would not result in a loss of sales so great as to offset the profits gained? Can the monopolist raise the price a little and not lose money by an offsetting reduction in sales? If so, then nonslip-grip hammers may be their own market. Noninfringing alternatives still may exist, but they are probably less likely than if the monopoly test fails. In other words, if the patent holder cannot pass this test by raising the price, then the patented good more likely faces competition from noninfringing alternatives. In our example, nonslip-grip hammers may be part of the larger hammer market, as some consumers who do not value the special grip will switch to other substitutes, such as the (now) even relatively cheaper regular hammers.

Economists wrestle mightily with market definition. In practical applications it requires accurate data demonstrating how consumers will respond. Although the market definition test is not dispositive—in part because of imprecise terminology (how small or significant, how long is nontransitory?)—it still may be helpful to examine what products satisfy the test. Can a product constrain price in a significant and non-transitory way? If so, then that product is in. We keep adding products and expanding the market definition until the answer is no. That relevant set of products gets us thinking again about acceptable alternatives.

Patent Review and Substitutes

Readers may be asking: But doesn't the patent review process itself determine if something is a substitute? The answer is yes, partially. The review of prior art helps eliminate what we might think of as the clearest substitute inventions. For example, in the case of a hammer, suppose that the nonslip-grip patent application specified a certain type of neoprene rubber, shaped into a mold to accommodate fingers. If the same type of grip had been patented for, say, garden implements, it could prevent the subsequent hammer grip patent application.

But setting aside this review of prior art, the patent process really cannot perform an economic analysis. There are substitutes in the public domain (plain hammers) and substitutes that might employ a noninfringing technology to achieve the same result—for instance, patented liquid hand-grip lotion used in combination with a regular hammer. (Both achieve the desired effect: the ability to hammer without losing one's grip.)

Because noninfringing substitutes almost always exist at the margin, patent attorneys usually seek to write the claimed structure of a patent as broadly as possible. Method patents are a different story. Sometimes the structure is patented by someone else or is in the public domain and someone gets a patent not on a structure itself but on the use of the structure (e.g., chemical Z used against solid tumors). In that context, a new use (chemical Z as hair regrowth cream) would not infringe the use patent, but still would infringe the structure patent, if one was still in force.

Back to Panduit

The third prong of the *Panduit* test concerns the capacity to capitalize on the patent. In a lawsuit, this criterion helps determine what percentage of the infringer's sales the patent holder reasonably could have expected to have made, had the infringing product not come into the marketplace. Outside of litigation, this criterion can go a long way in explaining the bargaining position of a patent holder whose patent is up for sale. Suppose that an individual inventor holds the hammer grip patent. Alone, he is unable to market and manufacture a hammer than incorporates his grip technology. Without landing a deal with a hammer manufacturer the patent is virtually worthless. However, now suppose that non-slip hammer manufacturer A is bargaining with another manufacturer, B. Further suppose that market studies have shown that consumers strongly prefer the patented grip that A sells. In this scenario, the patent would certainly be worth more.

The fourth criteria of the *Panduit* test contains the notion that the plaintiff needs to be able to provide a reasonably accurate estimate of the profits that would have been made had the infringement not taken place. If we extrapolate this concept to valuation, it is equivalent to saying "Projections for the profits attributable to this patent need to be reliable." Wild speculation of lost profits is not acceptable to a court; neither should it be to a good valuation. Projections that take into account historical performance, the riskiness of the cash flows, the financial condition of the company, and characteristics of the market are some of the ingredients required to do the valuation right.

Relating Panduit to the PIE-B

It is hoped that at this stage, readers can relate the *Panduit* criteria to PIE-B's dimensions: If demand for the asset is greater, economic benefit is greater. If there are no acceptable substitutes for the asset, then ownership of the benefits is more secure. (The opposite, of course, is that the features of the asset are not unique: Properties are shared by many owners.) If the owners of the asset can exploit demand, then economic benefit is greater. And, last, the less speculative a calculation of profit, the more certainly economic benefit can be calculated.

GEORGIA PACIFIC FACTORS

Sometimes the goal in litigation is to turn back the clock. We pretend that instead of one party infringing the patent of another party, the two parties would have entered into a *hypothetical negotiation* in which a *reasonable royalty* could be determined. Patent damages are deemed to be "not less than a reasonable royalty." This is the default measure. The framework routinely used in the analysis of patent damages are the so-called *Georgia Pacific* factors. In 1970, in *Georgia Pacific Corporation v. United States Plywood Corporation*, the court presented these 15 factors that it considered in determining what a reasonable royalty should be:

1. The royalties received by the patentee for the licensing of the patent in suit, proving or tending to prove an established royalty.
2. The rates paid by the licensee for the use of other patents comparable to the patent in suit.
3. The nature and scope of the license, as exclusive or nonexclusive, or as restricted or nonrestricted in terms of territory or with respect to whom the manufactured product may be sold.
4. The licensor's established policy and marketing programs to maintain the patent monopoly by not licensing others to use the invention or by granting licenses under special conditions designed to preserve that monopoly. (This factor traditionally tries to assign a value to a patent holder based on the holder's degree of protectiveness with respect to what may be protected under the patent. Put another way, if the owner

has shown a willingness to expend effort and money to protect its patent "monopoly," a higher hypothetical license fee may be proper. This factor looks to what the licensor has achieved with others in comparable circumstances.)

5. The commercial relationship between the licensor and licensee, such as whether they are competitors in the same territory in the same line of business, or whether they are inventor and promoter.
6. The effect of selling the patented specialty in promoting sales of other products of the licensee, the existing value of the invention to the licensor as a generator of sales of his or her nonpatented items, and the extent of such derivative or convoyed sales.
7. The duration of the patent and term of the license.
8. The established profitability of the product made under the patent, its commercial success, and its current popularity.
9. The utility and advantages of the patent property over the old modes or devices, if any, that had been used for working out similar results.
10. The nature of the patented invention, the character of the commercial embodiment of it as owned and produced by the licensor, and the benefits to those who have used the invention.
11. The extent to which the infringer has made use of the invention, and any evidence probative of the value of that use.
12. The portion of the profit or of the selling price that may be customary in the particular business or in comparable businesses to allow for the use of the invention or analogous inventions.
13. The portion of the realizable profit that should be credited to the invention as distinguished from the nonpatented elements, the manufacturing process, business risks, or significant features of improvements added by the infringer.
14. The opinion of qualified experts.
15. The amount that a willing licensor would have agreed to accept, and that a willing licensee would have agreed to pay at the time the infringement began.[2]

Some of these factors can be interpreted as overlapping with the economics of the *Panduit* criteria. Factor 8, for example, is a little like *Panduit* 1 and 4 together. *Georgia Pacific* 13 requires similar thinking to *Panduit* 2. It is the last factor—"the amount that a willing licensor would have agreed to accept, and that a willing licensee would have agreed to pay at the time the infringement began"—that captures the essence of the *Georgia Pacific* framework. It describes a world *but for* the patent infringement.

For example, suppose our hammer grip patent holder wants to charge a royalty of at least $1.00 per hammer. Suppose that the infringer has determined that a fee of $1.50 per hammer will wipe out any incremental profit. *Georgia Pacific* factor 15 tells us that a reasonable royalty must lie between $1.00 (the least the licensor is willing to take) and $1.50 (the most that the potential licensee would be willing to pay).

Exceptions

Interestingly, there can be some exceptions. Imagine that the infringing good is part of a bundle of goods—maybe the patent covers a certain socket wrench that is always sold as part of a set of socket wrenches. Then the upper bound on what the licensee may be willing to pay could be more than just the incremental profit on the particular wrench covered under the patent. The licensee will consider the overall increase in profit of the bundled goods—with the inclusion of the patented wrench—and compare that to the cost of the royalty. This actually relates to *Georgia Pacific* factor 6, which indicates that the promotional value or the value due to convoyed sales also should be considered in assigning a reasonable royalty.

Another exception is demonstrated by the case of the Black & Decker SnakeLights. Black & Decker sued an infringing manufacturer over patents covering its flexible flashlights. In this case, the court actually found that a reasonable royalty could exceed the selling price of the infringer's product. The results of this seemingly odd decision were explained by the lawyers and experts[3] in an article in the *Federal Circuit Bar Journal*. They introduced the idea that a reasonable royalty should be set to the patent owner's profit margin, if three conditions were met:

1. The infringed technology must be more valuable to the plaintiff than to the defendant. If this is true, then the groundwork is laid in a hypothetical negotiation such that the plaintiff patent holder has no economic incentive to license the technology. Why should the patent holder? He or she makes more profit by not sharing the patent. At what price would the patent holder become indifferent to licensing? This patent holder needs to get the price that achieves his or her own incremental profit margin. In the valuation context, this condition is important to be able to recognize. There are times when it makes sense not to license.
2. The plaintiff must meet the legal test for lost profits. This is similar to the third criteria of the *Panduit* test. If the plaintiff does not have the ability to make product that would supplant the infringing sales, then he or she could not have been damaged (at least that way). Again, relating this to valuation, we recognize that the value of a given patent is relative to its owner's ability to capitalize on it.
3. The defendant's sales must displace the plaintiff's on a one-for-one basis. In the case of SnakeLight, the plaintiffs were able to rely on this as a

rebuttable presumption. In valuation, or as defendants in a patent infringement suit, we would not be afforded this convenience. Rather, it would be our job to estimate how likely and how strong *displacement* would be. Remember our earlier discussion of the cross-price elasticity of demand? It returns again here as a way of determining displacement.

Relating Georgia Pacific to the PIE-B

Many of the economic underpinnings of the *Georgia Pacific* factors are, of course, related to PIE-B criteria. Readers are encouraged to think about how each of these factors reflects on ownership and economic benefits of some intangible asset. For example, consider the ninth factor: the utility and advantages of the patent property over the old modes or devices, if any, that had been used for working out similar results. The greater the utility, the greater the benefit. And by definition, if there are advantages, then ownership conveys benefits over nonowners.

TRADE SECRET FRAMEWORK

Trade secrets also have been considered by the courts under a framework that contains significant economic elements. Section 757 of the Restatement (First) of Torts (1939) prescribes six factors for determining whether something is a trade secret:

1. The extent to which the information is known outside the business
2. The extent to which the information is known within the company
3. The extent of measures taken to guard the secret
4. The value of the information
5. The resources expended on developing the information
6. The efforts required to duplicate the information

To place a trade secret somewhere along the two dimensions of the PIE-B, we examine these factors in combination. A trade secret that is not well known outside of the firm, that is heavily guarded, and that cost a great deal to create is an example of one that is strong on the ownership dimension. If the information also has demonstrable economic value, then the trade secret is strong along the benefits dimension as well.

FAMOUS DILUTION

As we touched on briefly in Chapter 2, the concept of trademark dilution was addressed recently by the Supreme Court in the Victoria's Secret matter. The

Court found for Victor's Little Secret, writing "There is a complete absence of evidence of any lessening of the capacity of the Victoria's Secret mark to identify and distinguish goods or services sold in Victoria's Secret stores or advertised in its catalogs." In the case, an army officer had been offended by an advertisement of Victor's Little Secret, but as the Court noted, the officer's conception of Victoria's Secret had not been changed. Had his conception of Victoria's Secret been changed (i.e., if he had thought that perhaps Victoria's Secret was now selling adult novelties as Victor's Little Secret had been), then dilution could have occurred. The 1995 Federal Trademark Dilution Act (FTDA) defines dilution as "the lessening of the capacity of a famous mark to identify and distinguish goods or services." Short of proof that capacity had been reduced, there can be no trademark dilution. Mere mental association of the junior mark with the famous mark is not enough.

This is interesting to us here because the criteria for whether a mark is distinctive and famous and the Court's dilution test both have a familiar economic ring. The FTDA's nonexclusive list for whether a mark is distinctive and famous is:

(A) The degree of inherent or acquired distinctiveness of the mark;
(B) The duration and extent of use of the mark in connection with the goods or services with which the mark is used;
(C) The duration and extent of advertising and publicity of the mark;
(D) The geographical extent of the trading area in which the mark is used;
(E) The channels of trade for the goods or services with which the mark is used;
(F) The degree of recognition of the mark in the trading areas and channels of trade used by the marks' owner and the person against whom the injunction is sought;
(G) The nature and extent of use of the same or similar marks by third parties; and
(H) Whether the mark was registered under the Act of March 3, 1881, or the Act of February 20, 1905, or on the principal register.

The 10 factors that the Second Circuit has developed to determine if dilution has occurred are:

1. Distinctiveness
2. Similarity of the marks
3. Proximity of the products and the likelihood of bridging the gap
4. Interrelationship among the distinctiveness of the senior mark, the similarity of the junior mark, and the proximity of the products

5. Shared consumers and geographic limitations
6. Sophistication of consumers
7. Actual confusion
8. Adjectival or referential quality of the junior use
9. Harm to the junior user and delay by the senior user
10. Effect of [the] senior's prior laxity in protecting the mark

By this time, readers will recognize the economic concepts of consumer preference, substitution, elasticity, and market definition in these legal guidelines.

SUMMARY

Litigation often is the place where intangible asset valuation is scrutinized most highly. When a party is seeking damages because it alleges that its intangible assets have been stolen, diluted, or misused, it will hire an expert to put a value on them. And because accused parties are interested in limiting their exposure, often they will hire a rebuttal expert to respond to the valuation. Many times these types of professional valuations are done within the economic frameworks outlined in the *Panduit* and/or *Georgia Pacific* cases. Many of the economic principles established therein provide excellent insight for valuing intangibles in nonlitigation matters too. In the next chapter, we take a look at some strategic implications of intangibles. Securitization plays a large role.

CHAPTER 10

Intangible Assets: Strategy and Securitization

So far we have discussed the economics of intangible assets, how the accounting rules treat them, and how the three basic valuation methodologies apply to intangibles. We have tried to capture these concepts with a simplifying framework that considers ownership and economic benefit as the two primary dimensions of value.

This chapter is about strategy—the strategy of turning proto-assets into intellectual property. In some management texts, this is described as the process of extracting value from intangible assets. The process is complicated, though. Intangible assets usually are not left lying about just waiting for a manager to pick them up and squeeze some productive value out of them. Nor are they created out of thin air despite the fact that we cannot touch them.

To examine strategies, we are going to return to the basics of the portfolio of intangible economic benefits (PIE-B). Identifying intangible assets will first on the list. Identification here is nearly synonymous with finding an asset's optimal use. (There is no morality implied—"optimal" simply means the most profitable use.) At center stage is the idea of *securitization*. We mean the term plainly: Securitizing intangibles means making intangibles more secure.[1]

This chapter's discussion is not meant to be exhaustive. Rather, the examples aim to provide some creative ideas of how proto-assets get converted into more secure intangibles. Some of the strategic aspects of securitization to be examined include:

- Identifying optimal use
- The dynamic nature of securitization
- Securing intellectual property through extension
- Securing off–balance sheet intangibles

As a case study, we will also examine what insecurity has meant in the recording industry.

BOWIE BONDS

In the context of a strategy for managing intangible assets, securitization does not have to mean creating an intangible asset-backed security for sale in the financial markets. It just means coming up with the old accounting standard: something that is identifiable and separable. Something identifiable is better able to be secured against theft, and something separable is better able to be packaged up for sale.

In 1997 the musician David Bowie made the securitization of intangible assets famous with a $55 million issuance of asset-backed bonds. The collateral was future royalties from some 25 albums Bowie recorded before 1990. (Prudential Insurance bought the bonds.) Bowie's creation so captured the imagination of investors that it gave birth to a generic term; "Bowie bonds" have come to mean any bond backed by intangible assets. These have included offerings in film and television, literary works, and games.[2] Although the Bowie bonds have fared poorly for their guarantor, the concept is not without merit.[3]

If the intangible asset already has been identified—if it is already some form of intellectual property—then securitizing it could mean adding more property definitions: for instance, extending a patent right into a brand. If the intangible is unidentified, then obviously, the first step is to find it. Relating this strategy to the PIE-B, securitizing intangibles is the equivalent of moving more and more proto-assets into the realm of identifiable intellectual property. Figure 10.1 depicts the process.

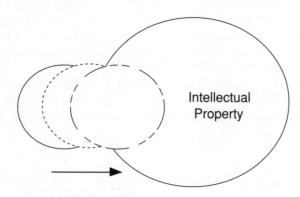

FIGURE 10.1   Proto Assets.

IDENTIFICATION

In the early 1970s, before Las Vegas was highly developed, Steve Winn (now a successful real estate and hotel developer) sold to Caesars Palace a narrow strip of land next to the hotel's parking lot for twice what he had paid only a few months before. Caesars was willing to pay such a premium because of the location of the parking lot—across the Las Vegas Strip from Caesars' hotel and casino.

The reason for Caesars' premium was that Winn had threatened to put a casino on the site. The world's narrowest casino would compete with Caesars Palace. That hidden value—the intangible asset—was not reflected in the price Winn had paid, but it was incorporated into the price that Caesars paid just a few months later.

The location in this case was not an intangible—location was inexorably tied to the dirt of the real property. So what accounts for the rapid increase in value? The land's optimal use had gone undetected by the owner before Winn.

"Location, location, location" may be the mantra in real estate, but the optimal use of the location is inseparable from its value. A different threat also might have held Caesars ransom (say, the threat to put a toxic dump on the property), but that threat might not be as credible in Las Vegas nor perhaps as costly to Caesars.

The strategic question is to ask: Is the asset being put to its optimal use? The land across from the Chicago Cubs Wrigley Field provides a more dynamic example, since the security (degree of ownership control) changed over time.

DYNAMIC SECURITIZATION

Wrigley Field is located in a mostly residential neighborhood. Not far over the right and left field wall are two streets (Sheffield and Waveland) on which mostly residential apartment buildings are located. For years residents of those apartment buildings had set up lawn chairs on their roofs in order to look into the ballpark. But in the last decade or so, some building owners decided to capitalize on their views. That is, they recognized that their buildings' locations provided them with an intangible asset: viewing rights.

Economic Benefit

Soon many of the rooftops sprouted bleachers as their owners set up businesses that charged admission for refreshments and access to the roofs. As buildings were bought and sold along Sheffield and Waveland, the intangible viewing rights became more important than the regular rental income from the apartments.

From our strategic perspective, watching the Cubs' games moved from a proto-asset into the realm of an identifiable intangible. Recognizing that the buildings could be used profitably for viewing the games meant that the highest and best use of the real estate now encompassed more than just residential purpose. Economic benefits, too, were soon quantifiable as the rooftop businesses built up a track record of their own attendance revenues.

Ownership

Not surprisingly, the Tribune Company, owners of the Cubs franchise, had a different view of the intangible asset. It was becoming more obvious that there were economic benefits to watching the games from across the streets. The Tribune Company sought to secure its ownership. It did this both through legal means (filing lawsuits) and by physically installing screens and other devices to prevent many fans on the rooftops from seeing into the stadium. As a result, the rooftop owners faced decreased security for the viewing rights. The degree of ownership was weakened, to use the PIE-B dimension. In addition, the uncertainty associated with ownership made the future cash flows more uncertain, too.

Eventually, the Tribune Company and the rooftop owners came to a settlement. The rooftop businesses agreed to pay a royalty to the team, and the Tribune Company agreed to drop its lawsuit and prevent any further obstruction of the view from outside Wrigley. In the end, the agreement securitized the asset for both parties. In addition to a royalty, the Tribune Company got the rooftop owners to recognize the Cubs had property rights that extended out across Waveland and Sheffield avenues. The rooftop owners, in return, were assured that (at least for now) the revenues associated with Cubs' watching would continue with relative stability. Figure 10.2 shows how, for the rooftop owners, the intangible's strength along the PIE-B's dimensions shifted considerably over time.

Portability

The Wrigley Field area rooftop owners certainly figured out a way to convert an obscure property right into a relatively secure intangible asset. But is it really intellectual property, the kind that can be bought and sold? The example is a little unsatisfactory. The rights associated with viewing the Cubs were identifiable and separable, and they could be quantified, too. But the rooftop owners cannot take the core concept—charging a fee to view a ball game from outside the ballpark—and use it anywhere else. A trade secret covering this, a method patent that describes this, or a service mark

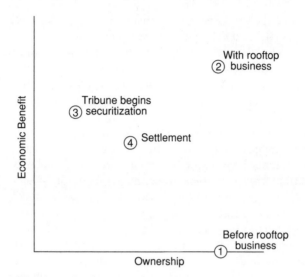

FIGURE 10.2   The Rooftops' View.

that proscribes the kind of activity all would fail miserably. Few would pay to use them because the idea is not very portable. Who would be willing to buy a book called *How to Profit from Stadium Viewing Rights—a Lesson from Wrigley Field*?

The lack of portability has a lot to do with how the intangible is consumed. When people can consume an intangible asset's benefits in many different forms (or, in this case, places), then generally the asset will be more valuable. (Recall our discussion of scalability and joint consumption from Chapter 3.) There is more opportunity to extend the property rights through branding and, presumably, a larger market interested in the property. Next we consider how expiring intangibles, mostly patents, are extended through their brand.

EXTENSION

Companies that have patented successful products all eventually face the music when their patents expire. The profits attract competition. This happens in all types of industries.

A now widely used brand strategy is to convert demand for the patented good into demand for the trademarked good. In this way, the brand extends ownership and economic benefit beyond what was possible with patented attributes. Trade dress covers color, shape, lettering, even smell. One example is the artificial sweetener Nutrasweet, a brand name for aspartame that went off patent in 1992. Although other makers of aspartame existed, none had seeded the market to raise consumer awareness for what was now perceived a brand, rather than a patented technology.

Another example is the drug Nexium. This is the brand name for AstraZeneca's acid reflux medicine, generically called esomeprazole. Astra-Zeneca launched a campaign that emphasized trade dress (the Little Purple Pill) to sustain its place in what was becoming a crowded market for acid reflux medicine.

Dolby Systems is also a good example. Dolby's most famous creation was a noise reduction system used in cassette tape duplication. Many of Dolby labs' patents have expired (along with the popularity of cassette tapes), but the name is associated with quality audio—hence its use in movie theater systems all over the world.

Although creative rights in copyrighted material are much longer than an inventor's rights in patent, copyrights also are extended through brand. Harry Potter audiotapes, CDs, and toys are valuable because the characters originally copyrighted in books are now included in copyrighted audiotapes, CDs, and movies; and, they are protected by trademarks on Halloween costumes, dolls, and candy.

OFF-BALANCE SHEET INTANGIBLES

Sometimes there are intangible assets associated with a firm's product that the firm may not explicitly control. These are prime candidates for some form of securitization. Online communities, hobbyist clubs, and dealer networks provide good examples.

Many clubs and online communities begin life as informal user groups. People with shared interests (many of them academic but not necessarily so) connect at periodic club meetings or perhaps via the Internet to discuss their passions or to vent their frustrations. Depending on their purpose, these forums could be considered off-balance sheet assets—or liabilities. In either case, if the forum discusses a company's product, that company should consider the intangible asset implications.

If vintage Porsche clubs exist, for example, then there are more parts, cars, repair tips, and general information available than without the clubs. There is greater Porsche liquidity, which reduces the costs of owning the car. These forces enhance the Porsche brand and all the intellectual property (patents, trademarks, trade secrets) that help build it. But there are forces working the other direction as well. The easier it becomes to own a vintage Porsche, the less attractive a new one may be. And the ability of irate Porsche owners to make themselves heard also can have a negative effect on the Porsche brand value.

Fears of slander and libel probably keep vehemently negative communities from gaining much ground. But good companies recognize the need to foster positive, supportive communities in order to be able to control the damage. Official Web sites are often the response to renegade ones.

In addition, such communities are often a way for firms to cut costs directly. For example, many firms provide a wealth of information for free on their Web sites in extensive lists of frequently asked questions (FAQs) and knowledge bases. Some hold corporate-sponsored live-chat and ask-the-expert events, both for consumption by their customers, but also to share knowledge within the firm. The idea of the value of online communities even gave birth to the business of online community management. One of the providers is Participate.com, which was formed in 1997 around the peak of Internet interest. Interestingly, Participate itself went through a process of securitization, shifting the firm's business model from being a services and consulting firm to being a software provider.

Off–balance sheet communities do not necessarily have to be made up of a company's customers. Supplier networks and dealer networks also might qualify, especially if they produce benefits without a direct investment from the company.

INSECURITY—THE CASE OF THE RECORDING INDUSTRY

What happens when intangibles become insecure? The story is currently unfolding in the recording industry, which provides us with some valuable insights.

Why Music?

This book has made frequent reference to intangibles in the entertainment industry generally and the music business, in particular. This is not accidental. The entertainment industries "grew up" with intangibles. And although music revenues are dwarfed by those of other core copyrighted industries, such as publishing and software, music has been at the forefront of the changing dynamics that technology has imposed on intangibles. The best explanation is actually pretty simple: Music is now largely digital, and digital music files are small enough to be distributed (legally and illegally) via the Internet. The same cannot be said for movies—yet.

Because of this position, the recording industry has faced technological attacks on its intellectual property faster perhaps than any other industry. Although it is true that software firms also face massive piracy threats, their property has been digital from the get-go. In this context, the record companies' challenge is unique. Examining their journey and the likely outcomes completes our analysis of securitization, or in this case, the lack of it.

Why Now?

The combined threat posed by the Internet, Napster, and the MP3 format was not the first major challenge to face the record industry. The fears voiced about the effect newly introduced high-quality cassette decks and digital audio tape recorders would have on record or CD sales sound all too familiar in the current context. Indeed, the Home Recording Act and the definition of fair use were arrived at long before MP3 existed.

However, this time it is different. Today the record industry must contend with not just a new format, but a new form of distribution and a new means of production. The fact that music can be shared (for profit or not) via the Internet generally, and through file-swapping software specifically, has serious economic ramifications for artists and labels. Consensus among artists, lawyers, economists and engineers is virtually impossible, but three conclusions are clear.

First, digital speed and space continue to expand rapidly (Moore's Law)—making rather shortsighted the argument that, in terms of sound or video quality, MP3s and video via the Internet are not good substitutes for "store-bought" CDs or DVDs. The "poor substitute" argument has all but vanished with respect to audio, but some video observers still make the claim. They will not be able to do so for long.

Second, adequate audio file protection methods—such as encryption sponsored by the Secure Digital Music Initiative (SDMI) have so far proven elusive. It is also clear that consumers expect that some amount of copying is permissible—for timeshifting, archiving, or use on different platforms.

Third, legislation against file-swapping may be ineffective or undesirable. Although surveys have shown that in just a couple of years, consumers' attitude toward illegal copying have swung around (from a majority thinking piracy is acceptable to a majority now thinking it wrong), hostless architecture and fragmented end users make the legal system a tricky enforcement tool. Moreover, findings of contributory liability (coming after the sites themselves) may dampen socially valuable innovation.

Insecure Future of the Labels

There is a future in online music sales, as Apple's iTunes has made abundantly clear. But at the same time, the network of file-sharing is likely to become more decentralized; and increases in bandwidth capacity may foster different technologies. What impact will there be on the supply of raw material, the intangible assets that the music industry needs? What implications does this have for the major record labels? Some consequences of insecurity follow.

Recording artists who can do so might switch away from recorded music and to live performance. This new product offering will not be possible for all artists, since some only record and others almost exclusively tour. Yet economic forces will drive artists toward investing in the best-protected (or least infringed) form of intellectual property. This could reduce the supply of raw material for record labels; so to attract artists, royalty rates may increase, which in turn might drive down label profitability.

In the face of rapidly improving sound quality over the Web, the royalties artists can earn from CD sales will decline. Mechanical royalties, too, could also largely be destroyed by file-swapping over the Internet. Although digital music streaming will be easier for performance rights organizations such as BMI and American Society of Composers, Authors, and Publishers (ASCAP) to monitor than FM radio, digital file-swapping is not.

An up-front royalty scheme might involve collecting fixed fees for artists on all legitimate music sales. "Bot" software could collect download data from commercial sites, with Napster itself (or something like it) becoming the Internet's BMI or ASCAP, allocating back the royalties collected on a proportional share of downloads. But bots also would have to register illegal activity—there is, of course, a propensity for hits to be pirated more than failures, so that more successful artists would have serious concerns about being undercompensated in this type of scheme.

In all cases, if piracy cannot effectively be prevented, then pricing for a legitimate recording must move toward the price of an acceptable substitute, which is, in any event, less than it has been. Repricing can probably be viewed as resulting in decreasing margins for the record companies. Consumers have shown that they are willing to pay *something* for legitimate, high-fidelity music, but it is less than the labels apparently thought.

Strategic Shift

Old habits die hard, and this is true for the record industry and consumers alike. It was not until 1991 that audio CD sales for the first time surpassed cassette sales. Even in 2000 sonically inferior cassette sales totaled $626 million. Until the last year or so, cassette players—not CD players—were standard equipment in most car audio systems.

Notwithstanding consumer entrenchment, the most important reason the major labels will not disappear is that the same technological advances that have threatened their very existence are also the forces that ensure their survival. The transfer of digital music via the Internet overwhelms consumers. Somebody must provide a floodgate. The market will still require "tastemakers" to help consumers cope with choice. The major labels still could fill this role.

There is precedent for a shift in the strategic focus of the major labels. Fifty years ago the labels served five functions: They discovered talent, matched talent to material, recorded songs, distributed records, and promoted artists. In the 1960s singer-songwriters such as Sam Cooke, the Beatles, Smokey Robinson, and Bob Dylan largely removed the matching function. Then, in the last 10 or 15 years, cheap digital recording technology largely removed the recording function; a major label recording budget was no longer necessary to make a quality record. The Internet now removes the distribution function, leaving the job of the labels to find and promote talent.

The long-run intellectual property of the record company, then, does not reside in its CDs or MP3s. Rather, it is firm-specific capital represented by the firm's ability to find and promote talent. Consumers will pay for that ability because it reduces their own search costs. What they will be buying is (presumably better) advice. What are the margins on advice? One only needs to look to corollary advice providers—MTV, VH-1, radio, newspapers, and magazines—to get some indication of the value of subscription services.

SUMMARY

This chapter described some of the strategies that make intangibles more secure. Identifying optimal use, extending intangibles' property characteristics, and identifying off–balance sheet intangibles all have the effect of moving more and more proto-assets into the realm of intellectual property. We also looked at some of the recent changes in the recording industry in order to probe intangible insecurity.

Some readers may feel disappointed that we have not arrived at a list of strategic recommendations, an easy to-do checklist, that would advise "patent all trade secrets" or "securitize all copyrights." The reason we cannot do this easily is that prescriptive rules for managing intangibles are no more valuable than those for tangible assets. Strategies and decisions about investment need to be informed by principles of economics and finance and they are governed by accounting. In this sense, all the preceding chapters combined give readers the guidance on what to do.

In the final chapter, we work a little on a theory to explain the "most" intangible assets of all, ephemeral assets such as charisma and beauty.

CHAPTER 11

Conclusion

In Chapter 1 we gave a quick nod to the concept that people have intangible assets, too. Then we talked some about the benefits of education and training, about how those were enhancements to individuals' balance sheets and also to firms that make investments in human capital. These intangibles are quantifiable to some degree—perhaps not always in terms of the benefits they ultimately produce, but more easily with regard to the costs. Tuition and training are usually hard numbers.

But not all economic benefit and its ownership or control flows from what can mostly be described as investments. In some sense, we still have missed the "really" intangible assets. Nowhere in this book have we described beauty, charisma, or other personality traits. Although it is true that one can invest in beauty and charisma, many beautiful and charismatic people are just born with it. People are often successful—that is, they create economic benefits—using these other qualities not covered by accounting rules. How can personality traits, the most ephemeral of intangible assets, be valued? How are those traits converted into something more secure? This chapter presents analysis of these most intangible of assets.

TOWARD A THEORY OF EPHEMERAL ASSETS

One way to begin our discussion of valuing ephemeral assets is to present an accounting framework. At the center of this framework is status.

Status

Status is defined as the stock of accumulated deference. When the stock gets large enough, we can afford to "sell" some off. Status is a little like cash—it is an asset itself, but it results from some arrangements of other assets, perhaps beauty, power, charisma, or athletic prowess. Status in this way signifies a securitization of personality traits. Although it is not as liquid as cash, status can be transferred apart from the underlying assets that created it.

Buyers acquire status in the hope that some "rubs off" and they can add it to their own personal balance sheet, but it has to be desirable in the social marketplace. For example, an obnoxious personality is unlikely to result in any accumulation of deference. There is not much of a market for obnoxiousness; for most people it is a repugnant human quality that creates no status.

To contrast, a "beautiful" painting may attract attention on looks alone. Most people achieve benefits just by viewing it. A beautiful Rembrandt painting may attract even more attention. If it is human nature to stock up on as much beauty as we can, it is also human nature to enhance one's status. For many people, owning a Rembrandt could serve both purposes.

Trading on Ephemerals

These types of intangible assets have their own history of securitization. Self-help gurus, supermodels, and ex-presidents can sell millions of books or magazines, or charge large appearance fees based on charisma, beauty, and wisdom. To be sure, most successful personalities also have more than a modicum of other valuable intangibles. Education and physical training are almost certainly also present in these examples. But still we find ourselves willing to pay extra to be associated with them. In fact, the stronger the association—the more likely some status will "rub off"—the more we are willing to pay. This explains why we pay only $100 a plate to attend a political fundraiser but might pay $500 to be invited to a more intimate gathering with a candidate. This is why buying a self-help book costs much less than attending a weeklong retreat with the self-help expert. In a week, our probability of absorbing status is much higher.

Interestingly, just as tangible assets become worn out and indefinitely lived intangibles become impaired, personality intangibles also can lose value. We need to be aware that it is possible to deplete our stock of status. This is what happens when celebrities are overexposed, when they start to be perceived as "hawking." Their status account is depleted, and the intangible asset that gave rise to their fame becomes impaired. In other words, there are consequences to opening one too many mini-malls.

There is an important notion of depth at work in the "sale" of ephemeral intangibles. A charismatic leader can widely disseminate some surface value, but if he offers up too much sage advice, enthusiasm, or financial pointers, he is no longer special; everyone will have his intangible. There are good reasons famous people often disguise their humble origins.

They fear that revealing too much about how they developed their ephemeral assets will deplete their status account. Rather than "patenting" their ephemerals, they keep them as trade secrets.

Valuing Ephemerals

At the heart of a valuation of ephemeral assets lies our basic construct of the portfolio of intangible benefits (PIE-B). The personal beauty of a model, for example, might be high up on the ownership dimension. How much that beauty is worth on the other side—economic benefit—depends on fashion trends. When "thin was in," supermodel Kate Moss could dominate the fashion pages. When "heavier" models became more fashionable, Ms. Moss's intangible asset became impaired.

Beauty can go the other way in the PIE-B, though. Suppose that blondes with blue eyes are in demand. That is to say, there is relatively more economic benefit to possessing those characteristics over, say, being red-haired and freckled. But being "blonde with blue eyes" is a weak intangible along the ownership dimension. There are a lot of blondes, many with blue eyes, and even more models willing to dye their hair or wear colored contacts.

This beauty intangible probably would be priced as a modeling fee. In general, valuation would be calculated using comparables (how much other models were recently paid), but the income approach also can make sense. The first year Cheryl Tiegs was on the cover of *Sports Illustrated*, her agent may have intuitively used comparables to negotiate her fee: How much was the "going rate" for a cover model? The second year, the incremental increase in circulation would have come into play in a fee negotiation.

SUMMARY

The title of this book describes not just the contents but the process, as well. Intangible assets, by their very definition, require extra steps to understand, to value, to securitize, to appreciate. It is true that the context matters for valuing all assets, but for intangibles, context takes on a dynamic characteristic: The boundaries of what constitutes an intangible are just not all that clear sometimes, and rarely do they remain static.

Let us return to the example presented in Chapter 6. Initially our goal was to determine if there was some intangible asset that Test Company owned as a result of the firm's soda machine. We decided that was going too far. We could not determine reliably the causal connection to the firm's higher productivity. That may have been corporate culture, or it may have been an investment in employee cross-training. We knew (actually we assumed for purposes of example) that there were economic benefits. But in the end we could not pin down what intangible asset produced them.

In our example, Test Company's chief executive could not fully securitize his firm's corporate culture, primarily because he could not attribute economic benefits to something separate and identifiable. He also could not sell corporate culture without selling the firm or somehow leasing the employees *en masse*. This does not mean, though, that the intangible did not exist. Nor does it mean that the executive could not take steps to enhance it. Such steps could make corporate culture more secure. Indeed, keeping the soda machine in Test Company's break room was just that kind of step.

Additional Resources

For additional information on the music industry's current situation, readers will find the following articles and studies informative:

"The Attack on Peer-to-Peer Software Echoes Past Efforts," *New York Times*, John Schwartz (Sept. 22, 2003), p. C3.

"A Battle Royal Over Internet Royalties," *National Journal*, Drew Clark (Dec. 14, 2002).

"Can the Record Business Survive?" *The New Yorker*, John Seabrook (July 7, 2003), p. 42.

"For Music Industry, U.S. Is Only the Tip of a Piracy Iceberg," *New York Times*, Mark Landler (Sept. 26, 2003), p. A1.

"It's All Free," *Time Magazine*, Grossman, Lev, et al, (May 5, 2003), p. 60.

"A Nation of Pirates," *U.S. News & World Report*, Kenneth Terrell and Seth Rosen (July 14, 2003), p. 40.

"Who Owns Ideas: The War Over Global Intellectual Property," *Foreign Affairs*, David Evans (November-December 2002).

"Will MP3 Downloads Annihilate the Record Industry?; The Evidence So Far," Stan Liebowitz, www.utdallas.edu/~liebowit/intprop/records.pdf, (June 2003).

In addition, the web sites of the Recording Industry Association of America (RIAA) http://www.riaa.com/default.asp, and the National Music Publishers of America (NMPA) http://www.nmpa.org/ provide additional information.

Notes

CHAPTER 1   Introducing Intangibles

1. *Merriam-Webster's Collegiate Dictionary*, 10th ed. (Springfield, MA: Merriam-Webster, 2001).
2. Ronald H. Coase, "The Nature of the Firm," *Economica* (November 1937), vol. 4: p. 386–405.

CHAPTER 2   History and Taxonomy

1. *Merriam-Webster's Collegiate Dictionary*, 10th ed. (Springfield, MA: Merriam-Webster, 2001).
2. Financial Accounting Standards Board, Original Pronouncements, *Accounting Standards*, vol. 2, (Norwalk, CT: FASB, June 1999) CON6, par. 25.
3. Statistics from http://www.patstats.org/2002.html.
4. Information on patent offices obtained from http://world.std.com/obi/Patents/Documents/GAO-japan-patent-report.
5. Information on obtaining a patent obtained from http://www.nwfusion.com/news/2000/0703patent.html?
6. See U.S. Code Title 35, Section 171, Patents for Design, http://www4.law.cornell.edu/uscode/35/171.html.
7. See U.S. Code Title 35, Section 101, Inventions Patentable, http://www4.law.cornell.edu/uscode/35/101.html.
8. The author, in fact, has been a consultant on these matters.
9. Information on copyrights obtained from http://www.copyright.gov/circs/circ1.html.
10. Congressional Budget Office, *Copyright Issues in Digital Media*, www.cbo.gov/showdoc.cfm?index-5738&sequence=0 (August 2004), Page x.
11. *Metropolitan-Goldwyn-Mayer Studios, Inc. v. Grokster, Ltd.*, CV 01-08541-SVW (PJWx), CV 01-09923-SVW (PJWx), 2003 U.S. Dist. LEXIS 6994 (C.D. Cal. Apr. 25, 2003).
12. National Conference of Commissioners on Uniform State Laws, *Uniform Trade Secrets Act* (Minneapolis, MN: NCCUSL, August 2–9, 1985), p. 6.
13. David D. Friedman, William M. Landes, and Richard A. Posner, "Some Economics of Trade Secret Law," *Journal of Economic Perspectives*. 5, no. 1 (1991): 61–72.
14. See David Silverstein, "Will Pre-Grant Patent Publication Undermine United States Trade Secret Law?" American Intellectual Property Law Association Quarterly Journal 23, no. 4 (Fall 1995): 695.

15. Tom Blackett, "What Is a Brand?" in *Brands and Branding*, Rita Clifton and John Simmons, eds., Princeton, NJ: Bloomberg Press, 2003), pp. 18–19.
16. Michael J. Cooper, Orlin Dimitrov, and P. Raghavendra Rau, "A Rose.com by Any Other Name," *Journal of Finance* 56(201): 2371–2388, p. 1.
17. Richard Sandomir, "At (Your Name Here) Arena, Money Talks," *New York Times*, May 30, 2004. The information was collected by the Bonham Group, a Denver-based sports marketing firm.
18. Gary Becker, 1993. *Human Capital: A Theoretical and Empirical Analysis, with Special Reference to Education* (Chicago: University of Chicago Press, 1993), pp. 15–16.
19. Thanks to Claire Anderson for posing the first question and to Professor Dana Northcut for posing the second.
20. FAS 5, Appendix C, Footnote 11: American Accounting Association, *Accounting and Reporting Standards for Corporate Financial Statements and Preceding Statements and Supplements* (Sarasota, FL: American Accounting Association, 1975), p. 16.

CHAPTER 3   Theory of and Research on Intangible Assets

1. International Federation of the Phonograph Industry, *Commercial Piracy Report*, 2004.
2. Ernan Haruvy, Vijay Mahajan, and Ashutosh Prasad, "The Effect of Piracy on the Market Penetration of Subscription Software," *Journal of Business* 77 (2004): S81–108.
3. Carl Diorio, " 'King' Poised to Ring Up $1 Bil Worldwide," *Daily Variety Gotham*, February 17, 2004, 51.
4. This is the average theatrical cost for members of The Motion Picture Association of America (MPAA). MPA Worldwide Market Research, *U.S. Entertainment Industry: 2003 MPA Market Statistics*.
5. Sherwin Rosen, "The Economics of Superstars," *American Economic Review* 71 (1981): 845–858.
6. Leonard Nakamura, "A Trillion Dollars a Year in Intangible Investment and the New Economy," in John Hand and Baruch Lev, eds., *Intangible Assets: Values, Measures, and Risks*, (Oxford: Oxford University Press, 2003).
7. Margaret Blair, and Steven Wallman, "The Growing Intangibles Reporting Discrepancy," *Unseen Wealth: Report of the Brookings Task Force on Intangibles* (Washington, DC: Brookings Institute Press, 2001). Reprinted in Hand and Lev, eds., *Intangible Assets: Values, Measures, and Risks*.
8. eBay Annual Report, 2003.
9. IBM Form 10-K and Annual Reports, 1993 and 2003.
10. James Tobin, "A General Equilibrium Approach to Monetary Theory," *Journal of Money, Credit and Banking* 1 (1969): 15–29.
11. K. H. Chung, and S. W. Pruitt, "A Simple Approximation of Tobin's q," *Financial Management* (Autumn 1994) pp. 70–74.

12. Kevin M. Murphy, and Finis Welch, "Wage Differentials in the 1990s: Is the Glass Half Full or Half Empty?" in Finis Welch, ed., *The Causes and Consequences of Increasing Inequality* (Chicago: University of Chicago Press, 2001).
13. Jacob Mincer, "Investment in U.S. Education and Training," National Bureau of Economic Research Working Paper No. 4844 (Cambridge, MA: NBER, August 1994).
14. Sam S. Atkins, "The 2004–2008 US Corporate Learning Technology Market. The New Corporate Learning Ecosystem: Disruptive Technologies and Outsourcing Dislodge First-Generation Products," Workflow Institute Analysis, July 12, 2004.
15. Louis K. C. Chan, Josef Lakonishok, and Theodore Sougiannis, "The Stock Market Valuation of Research and Development Expenditures," National Bureau of Economic Research Working Paper No. W7223 (Cambridge, MA: NBER, June 1999).
16. John Hand, "The Increasing Returns-to-scale of Intangibles," in *Intangible Assets: Values, Measures, and Risks*.
17. Murphy and Welch, "Wage Differentials in the 1990s."
18. Mincer, "Investment in U.S. Education and Training."
19. Lynne G. Zucker, Michael R. Darby, and Marilynn B. Brewer, "Intellectual Human Capital and the Birth of the US Biotechnology Enterprises," *American Economic Review* 88 (1988): 290–306.
20. Zhen Deng, Baruch Lev, and Francis Narin, "Science and Technology as Predictors of Stock Performance," *Financial Analysts Journal* (May/June 1999); reprinted in Hand and Lev, eds., *Intangible Assets: Values, Measures, and Risks*.
21. Chandrakanth Seethamraju, "The Value Relevance of Trademarks," in Hand and Lev. eds., *Intangible Assets: Values, Measures, and Risks*.
22. Kevin J. Murphy, "Executive Compensation," In Orley Ashenfelter and David Card, eds., *Handbook of Labor Economics* (Elsevier, North Holland, 1999) vol. 3B, Chap. 38.
23. Ibid.
24. Sherwin Rosen, "Authority, Control, and the Distribution of Earnings, *Bell Journal of Economics* 13 (1982): 311–323.
25. Robert Hall, "E-Capital: The Link Between the Stock Market and the Labor Market in the 1990s," *Brookings Papers on Economic Activity* 2 (2000): 73–102.

CHAPTER 4   Accounting for Intangibles

1. General Motors, SEC Form 10-K, Note 9 to the Consolidated Financial Statements, December 31, 2001.
2. General Motors, SEC Form 10-K, December 31, 2002.
3. Financial Accounting Standards Board, SFAS No. 142: *Goodwill and Other Intagible Assets* (Norwalk, CT: FASB, June 2001), par. 23.
4. Accounting Principles Board, *Opinion 17: Intangibles* (New York: American Institute of Certified Public Accountants, August 1970).

5. Financial Accounting Standards Board, *SFAS No. 141: Business Combinations* (Norwark, CT: FASB, June 2001) p. 27, section A12.
6. Ibid., p. 26, section A10.
7. American Institute of Certified Public Accountants, Accounting Principles Board, *Opinion 17: Intangibles* (New York: AICPA, August 1970), par. 1.
8. "Goodwill and Other Intangible Assets," (Norwalk, CT: FASB 2003), par. 109.
9. Ibid.
10. Ibid.
11. Financial Accounting Standards Board, SFAS No. 144: Accounting for the Impairment or Disposal of Long-Lived Assets (Norwalk, CT: FASB August 2001), par. 143, p. 9. It is not surprising that these events are taken from the FASB section on long-lived assets. They are not specific to intangibles: "A long-lived asset (asset group) shall be tested for recoverability whenever events or changes in circumstances indicate that its carrying amount may not be recoverable" Section 108, par. 143]
12. "Goodwill and Other Intangible Assets," par. 117.
13. Ibid., par. 128.
14. Ibid., par. 132.
15. FAS 142, *Goodwill and Other Intangible Assets,* par. 20.
16. Ibid., par. 21.
17. Financial Accounting Standards Board, *SFAS No 50: Financial Reporting in the Records and Music Industry* (Norwalk, CT: FSAB, November 1981), par. 11.
18. Dennis J. Chambers, Ross Jennings, and Robert B. Thompson, "Evidence on the Usefulness of Capitalizing and Amortizing Research and Development Costs," Current Draft, April 2000.
19. Baruch Lev, *Intangibles: Management, Measurement, and Reporting* (Washington, DC: Brookings Institution Press, 2001), p. 103.
20. Ibid, p. 89.
21. Pfizer Financial Report 2003, p. 5.
22. Financial Accounting Standards Board, *SFAS No. 50: Financial Reporting in the Record and Music Industry* (Norwalk, CT: FASB, November, 1981), par. 11.
23. Financial Accounting Standards Board, *SFAS No. 53: Financial Reporting by Producers and Distributors of Motion Picture Films* (Norwalk, CT: FASB December, 1981) Appendix A, Production Costs.

CHAPTER 5   Portfolio of Intangible Economic Benefits

1. The influential English scholar, Carol LeSeure pointed out long ago that there is almost always a better word to use than "thing." In this case, though, "thing" is exactly the right choice. The things up for review for inclusion or not in the PIE-B are still too nebulous to determine if they are assets, much less proto-assets.
2. Statistics from the National Association of Independent Colleges and Universities, www.naicu.edu/news/qkfacts.shtml.
3. The calculation is $6,000 per year, discounted at 3 percent for inflation.

4. Gary Becker, *Human Capital: A Theoretical and Empirical Analysis, with Special Reference to Education* (Chicago: University of Chicago Press, 1993), p. 20.
5. Gretchen Morgenson, "Explaining (or Not) Why the Boss Is Paid So Much," *New York Times*, January 25, 2004.
6. Nick Liddell, "The Valuation of Pharmaceutical Brands," In Tom Blackett and Rebecca Robins, eds., *Brand Medicine: The Role of Branding in the Pharmaceutical Industry* (New York: Palgrave, 2001).
7. Danish Agency for Trade and Industry, *Guideline for Intellectual Capital Statements* (Copenhagen: Ministry of Trade and Industry, November, 2000).
8. Baruch Lev, *Intangibles: Management, Measurement, and Reporting* (Washington, DC: Brookings Institution Press, 2001).

CHAPTER 6 Income Approach and Intangibles

1. Thanks to Rob Vishny at the University of Chicago for making this a priority in my own work.
2. Statistics from http://www.cbsnews.com/stories/2003/04/18/60minutes/main 550102.shtml.
3. Kate Zernike, "Fight against Fat Shifting to the Workplace," *New York Times*, October 12, 2003.
4. The article cites Forrester Research in stating the 15 percent drop: http://www. taipeitimes.com/News/biz/archives/2004/02/23/2003099856.
5. This is definitely an oversimplification. Sports contracts, music contracts, and film contracts are not likely to be exercisable on only one date. But for the purposes of example, complicating the options pricing model is not really necessary.
6. There can be serious shortcomings to using the Black-Scholes model for real options pricing; nontradable equity options and a mismatch between the option and the underlying asset are two that immediately come to mind.
7. Fischer Black and Myron Scholes, "The Pricing of Options and Corporate Liabilities," *Journal of Political Economy* 81 (1973): 637–654.

CHAPTER 7 Market Approach and Intangibles

1. For simplicity, we also will ignore the possibility that the acquirer paid a control premium for either acquisition.

CHAPTER 8 Cost Approach and Intangibles

1. The author has consulted to the United States Department of Justice in the thrift matters.
2. In the FIRREA cases, there are actually several different theories of damages. Restitution—"making one whole"—often was used to describe what I have called replacing the success the thrifts would have had, but for the government's breach of contract.

3. Miller, Merton, and Franco Modigliani, "The Cost of Capital, Corporation Finance, and the Theory of Investment." *American Economic Review* 48 (June 1958): 261–97.

CHAPTER 9 Intangible Assets and Litigation

1. *Georgia-Pacific Corporation v. United States Plywood Corporation*, Civ. A. No. 99-195, 318 F. Supp. 1116; 1970 U.S. Dist. LEXIS 11541; 166 U.S.P.Q. (BNA) 235 (May 28, 1970).
2. See Jonathan Arnold, Anita Garten, John Janka, and Raymond Niro, "The Law and Economics of Reasonable Royalty Damages after Black & Decker's 'SnakeLight' Litigation," *Federal Circuit Bar Journal* 7, no. 4 (Winter 1997): 373–390.

CHAPTER 10 Intangible Assets: Strategy and Securitization

1. This more generic use of the word "securitize" is nicely described in a paper written by James Conley and John Szobocsan: "Snow White Shows the Way," *Managing Intellectual Property*, (2001).
2. For a good current overview on Bowie bonds, see Roy Davies's Web site, "Who's Who in Bowie Bonds," http://www.ex.ac.uk/~RDavies/arian/bowiebonds.html#stars.
3. Intellectual property securitizations are not yet popular with insurers. As my colleague Chris Culp points out, issues of adverse selection arise, and the insurers are none too keen to underwrite primary or core risk. This is also why most pharmaceutical patent offerings have fared poorly.

References

Atkins, Sam S. The 2004-2008 US Corporate Learning Technology Market. *The New Corporate Learning Ecosystem: Disruptive Technologies and Outsourcing Dislodge First-Generation Products*. Workflow Institute Analysis. July 12, 2004.

Becker, Gary. *Human Capital: A Theoretical and Empirical Analysis, with Special Reference to Education*. Chicago: University of Chicago Press, 1993.

Black, Fischer, and Myron Scholes. "The Pricing of Options and Corporate Liabilities." *Journal of Political Economy* 81 (1973): 637–654.

Blackett, Tom. "What Is a Brand?" In *Brands and Branding*. Edited by Rita Clifton and John Simmons. Princeton, NJ: Bloomberg Press, 2003.

Blackett, Tom, and Rebecca Robins, Eds. Brand Medicine: *The Role of Branding in the Pharmaceutical Industry*. New York: Palgrave, 2001.

Blair, Margaret, and Steven Wallman. "The Growing Intangibles Reporting Discrepancy." *Unseen Wealth: Report of the Brookings Task Force on Intangibles*. Washington, DC: Brookings Institute Press, 2001. Reprinted in *Intangible Assets: Values, Measures, and Risks*. Edited by John Hand and Baruch Lev. Oxford: Oxford University Press, 2003.

Chambers, Dennis J., Ross Jennings, and Robert B. Thompson. *Evidence on the Usefulness of Capitalizing and Amortizing Research and Development Costs*. Current Draft, April 2000.

Chan, Louis K. C., Josef Lakonishok, and Theodore Sougiannis. "The Stock Market Valuation of Research and Development Expenditures." National Bureau of Economic Research Working Paper No. W7223, June 1999.

Chung, K. H., and S. W. Pruitt. "A Simple Approximation of Tobin's q," *Financial Management*. Autumn 1994, pp. 70–74.

Coase, Ronald H. "The Nature of the Firm," *Economica*, 4 (1937): 386–405.

Congressional Budget Office. *Copyright Issues in Digital Media*, Washington, DC: Congressional Budget Office, August 2004.

Conley, James, and John Szoboscan. "Snow White Shows the Way." *Managing Intellectual Property*, 2001.

Cooper, Michael J., Orlin Dimitrov, and P. Raghavendra Rau. "A Rose.com by Any Other Name." *Journal of Finance* 56 (2001): 2371–2388.

Deng, Zhen, Baruch Lev, and Francis Narin. "Science and Technology as Predictors of Stock Performance." *Financial Analysts Journal* (May/June 1999). Reprinted in *Intangible Assets: Values, Measures, and Risks*. Edited by John Hand and Baruch Lev. Oxford: Oxford University Press, 2003.

eBay Annual Report 2003.

Exposure Draft Proposed Statement of FAS *Fair Value Measurements,* Norwalk, CT: FASB, June 2004 No. 1201-100, June 23, 2004.

Financial Accounting Standards Board Original Pronouncements, *Accounting Standards,* Norwalk, CT: FASB, June 1999 vol. 2, CON6, par. 25.

Financial Accounting Standards Board. *Section G40: Goodwill and Other Intangible Assets.* Current Text 2003/2004: Accounting Standards. Norwalk, CT: FASB, 2003.

Financial Accounting Standards Board. *SFAS No. 144: Accounting for the Impairment or Disposal of Long-Lived Assets.* Norwalk, CT: FASB, August 2001, par. 143.

Financial Accounting Standards Board. *SFAS No. 50: Financial Reporting in the Record and Music Industry.* Norwalk, CT: FASB, November 1981, par. 11.

Foster, George. *Financial Statement Analysis,* 2nd ed. Englewood Cliffs, NJ: Prentice-Hall, 1986.

Friedman, David D., William M. Landes, and Richard A. Posner. Some Economics of Trade Secret Law." *Journal of Economic Perspectives 5,* no. 1 (1991): 61–72.

Hall, Robert. "E-Capital: The Link Between the Stock Market and the Labor Market in the 1990s." *Brookings Papers on Economic Activity 2* (2000): 73–102.

Hand, John. "The Increasing Returns-to-scale of Intangibles." In *Intangible Assets: Values, Measures, and Risks.* Edited by John Hand and Baruch Lev. Oxford: Oxford University Press, 2003.

Hand, John, and Baruch Lev, Eds. *Intangible Assets: Values, Measures, and Risks.* Oxford: Oxford University Press, 2003.

Haruvy, Ernan, Vijay Mahajan, and Ashutosh Prasad. "The Effect of Piracy on the Market Penetration of Subscription Software." *Journal of Business* 77 (2004): S81–108.

IBM Form 10-K and Annual Report, 1993 and 2003.

International Federation of the Phonograph Industry, *Commercial Piracy Report,* 2004.

Lev, Baruch. 2001. *Intangibles: Management, Measurement, and Reporting.* Washington, DC: Brookings Institution Press.

Liddell, Nick. "The Valuation of Pharmaceutical Brands." In *Brand Medicine: The Role of Branding in the Pharmaceutical Industry.* Edited by Tom Blackett and Rebecca Robins. New York: Palgrave, 2001.

Merriam-Webster's Collegiate Dictionary, 10th ed. Springfield, MA: Merriam-Webster, 2001.

Miller, Merton, and Franco Modigliani. "The Cost of Capital, Corporate Finance, and the Theory of Investment." *American Economic Review* 48 (June 1958): 261–297.

Mincer, Jacob. "Investment in U.S. Education and Training." National Bureau of Economic Research Working Paper No. 4844, Cambridge, MA: NBER, August 1994.

Murphy, Kevin J. "Executive Compensation." Edited by Orley Ashenfelter and David Card in *Handbook of Labor Economics.* Elsevier, North Holland, 1999, vol. 3B, Chap. 3B.

Murphy, Kevin M., and Finis Welch. "Wage Differentials in the 1990s: Is the Glass Half Full or Half Empty?" In *The Causes and Consequences of Increasing Inequality*. Edited by Finis Welch. Chicago: University of Chicago Press, 2001.

Nakamura, Leonard. "A Trillion Dollars a Year in Intangible Investment and the New Economy." Edited by John Hand and Baruch Lev in *Intangible Assets: Values, Measures, and Risks*. Oxford: Oxford University Press, 2003.

Podolny, J. M., and D. J. Phillips. "The Dynamics of Organizational Status." *Journal of Industrial and Corporate Change*, 5 1996: 453–471.

Rosen, Sherwin. "The Economics of Superstars." *American Economic Review* 71 (1981): 845–858.

Rosen, Sherwin. "Authority, Control, and the Distribution of Earnings." *Bell Journal of Economics* 13 (1982): 311–323.

Seethamraju, Chandrakanth. "The Value Relevance of Trademarks." Edited by John Hand and Baruch Lev in *Intangible Assets: Values, Measures, and Risks*. Oxford: Oxford University Press, 2003.

Smith, Gordon V., and Russell L. Parr. *Valuation of Intellectual Property and Intangible Assets*, 3rd ed. John Wiley & Sons, NY: 2000.

Tobin, James. "A General Equilibrium Approach to Monetary Theory." *Journal of Money, Credit and Banking* 1 (1969): 15–29.

U.S. Department of Justice and the Federal Trade Commission, *Horizontal Merger Guidelines*, www.usdoj.gov/atr/public/guidelines/horiz.book/hmgl.html. Issued April 2, 1992, revised April 8, 1997.

Zucker, Lynne G., Michael R. Darby, and Marilynn B. Brewer. "Intellectual Human Capital and the Birth of the US Biotechnology Enterprises." *American Economic Review* 88 (1988): 290–306.

Index

ABOUT THE AUTHOR

Jeffrey Cohen is a Principal of Chicago Partners, an economics, accounting, and finance consulting firm that specializes in the application of those disciplines in legal and regulatory matters. Mr. Cohen is also the Director of the firm's intellectual property practice.

Mr. Cohen has nearly 18 years of experience consulting to Fortune 100 companies, the nation's top law firms, and various government agencies. He has directed analysis in the areas of intellectual property, antitrust, securities, bankruptcy, and valuation and has testified on damages in litigation.

Much of Mr. Cohen's work is in technology-intensive industries, including software and entertainment. This focus grows out of his lifetime career as a professional musician. A critically acclaimed songwriter, Mr. Cohen has performed popular music throughout the country.

Mr. Cohen was educated at the University of Chicago, where he received both his B.A. and M.B.A. degrees. He lives in Chicago with his wife and two children.